Tobias Sm

William Henry Oliphant Smeaton

Alpha Editions

This edition published in 2023

ISBN : 9789362097958

Design and Setting By
Alpha Editions
www.alphaedis.com
Email - info@alphaedis.com

Contents

CHAPTER I

'Every successful novelist must be more or less a poet, even though he may never have written a line of verse. The quality of imagination is absolutely indispensable to him.... Smollett was a poet of distinction!'

Such was the estimate formed by Sir Walter Scott—one of the most incisive and sympathetic critics that ever pronounced judgment—of the element of inspiration in every great writer of fiction. Experimentally conscious of what was of value in his own case,—himself the great Wizard of Fiction,—he would reason by analogy what would be of power to inspire other men. If the poetic faculty were indispensable for the production of *The Heart of Midlothian* and *Ivanhoe*, equally would it be needed in *Peregrine Pickle* and *Humphrey Clinker*. That the poetic stimulus is the most powerful of all, is a truth that has been remarked times and oft. That it forms the true key to unlock the otherwise elusive and self–centred character of Tobias George Smollett, has not, I think, previously been noted.

To write Smollett's life with absolute impartiality is more than ordinarily difficult. The creator of *Roderick Random* was one for whom a generous charity would require to make more allowances than man is commonly called upon to make for man. Actions and utterances that might be and were mistaken for irritation and shortness of temper, were in reality due to the impatience of genius, chafing under the restrictions laid upon it by the mental torpor or intellectual sluggishness of others. The eagle eye of his genius perceived intuitively what other men generally attain only as the result of ratiocinative process. Smollett has unjustly been characterised as bad–tempered, choleric, supercilious, and the like, simply because the key was lacking to his character. Far indeed from being any of these was he. Impatient without doubt he was, but by no means in larger measure than Carlyle, Tennyson, Dickens, Goethe, or Schiller, and the feeling is wrongly defined as impatience. It is rather the desire to give less intellectually nimble companions a fillip up in the mental race, that they may not lag so far behind as to make intercourse a martyrdom.

Smollett's distinguishing characteristic in the great gallery of eighteenth–century novelists was his exhaustless fertility. In his four great novels, *Roderick Random*, *Peregrine Pickle*, *Ferdinand Count Fathom*, and *Humphrey Clinker*, he has employed as many incidents, developed as many striking situations, and utilised as many happily conceived accidents of time and place, as Richardson, Fielding, Sterne, Henry Mackenzie, and Mrs. Radcliffe put together. His invention is marvellously fertile, and as felicitous as fertile. He makes no attempt to excel in what may be termed the 'architectonic' faculty, or the symmetrical evolution and interweaving of plot. Incident succeeds incident, fact follows fact, and scene, scene, in the most bewildering profusion. There is a prodigality visible, nay, an intellectual waste, indicative of an imaginative wealth almost unique since the days of Homer. By some critics, following in the footsteps of Sir Walter Scott, a curious vagary has been rendered fashionable of introducing the method of comparative analysis into every literary judgment. In place of declaring in plain, straightforward terms the reason why they either admire or censure the works of a man of genius, they must now drag in somebody else, with whom he is supposed to present points of affinity or contrast, and they glibly descant on the attributes wherein the author under consideration surpasses or falls short of his rival, what elements and qualities of style the one possesses which the other lacks, until in the end the reader is thoroughly befogged to know which is which and who is who. The higher criticism has its place in literary judgments as well as in theological, and the change is not for the better.

Tobias George Smollett resembled William Shakespeare in one respect if in no other—that a doubt exists as to the precise date of his birth. The first mention made of the future novelist occurs in no birth register that is known to exist, but in the parish record of baptisms in connection with the parochial district of Cardross. Therein, under the date 19th March 1721, we read: 'Tobias George, son to Mr. Archd. Smollett and Barbara Cunningham, was baptised.' The day in question was a Sunday, and, as Robert Chambers very properly remarks, 'it may be inferred that the baptism took place, according to old Scottish fashion, in the parish kirk.' This tentative inference may be changed into certainty when we recall the strict Presbyterianism of his grandfather's household, in whose eyes such an injunction as the following, taken from *The Directory for the Public Worship of God*, established by Act of General Assembly and Act of Parliament in 1645, would be as sacredly binding as the laws of the Medes and Persians:—'Baptism, as it is not unnecessarily to be delayed, so it is not to be administered in any case by any private person, ... nor is it to be administered in private places or privately, but in the place of public worship and in the face of the congregation.'

So much for the baptism. Now for the date of birth. Here only second–hand evidence is forthcoming. In one of the unpublished letters of John Home, author of *Douglas*, which it was recently my fortune to see, he mentions a walk which Smollett and he had taken together during the visit of the latter to London, when trying to get his first play, *Agis*, accepted by the theatrical managers. During the course of the walk Smollett mentioned the fact that his birthday had been celebrated two days before. The date of their meeting was the 18th March 1750. If reliance can be placed on this roundabout means of arriving at a fact, Smollett's birth took place on the 16th March 1721.

Genealogies are wearisome. Readers who desire to trace the family of the Smolletts back to the sixteenth century can do so with advantage in the Lives of Moore, Herbert, and Chambers. Our purpose is with the novelist himself, not with his ancestors to the fourth and fifth generations. Suffice it to say that Tobias George Smollett was the son of Archibald, fourth son of Sir James Smollett of Bonhill, a Dumbartonshire estate situated amidst the romantic scenery of the Vale of Leven, and in the vicinity of the queen of Scottish lakes, Loch Lomond.

Sir James Smollett, a stern old Whig of the Revolution type, to whom 'Prelacy was only less tolerable than Popery, and the adherents of both deserve hanging,' had risked property, prospects, and life at the time when James VII. staked his dynasty against a mass—and lost. So prominent was the part Sir James Smollett took in influencing public sentiment in favour of William and Mary, even while one of the Commissaries or Consistorial Judges of Edinburgh, that the grateful monarch knighted him, and the Earl of Argyll appointed him deputy–lieutenant of Dumbartonshire.

A very different character was the novelist's father. Archibald Smollett seems to have been, in Scots parlance, 'as *feckless* as his father was *fitty*.' The characteristic of the rolling stone was pre–eminently his. Consequently, as regards moss, in the shape of worldly gear, he gathered not a stiver unto him. But that did not trouble him. Like Charles Surface, his distresses were so many that the only thing he could not afford to part with was his good spirits, which, by the same token, chanced to be the only *good* thing he had about him. His health was bad, his morals were bad, his prospects were bad,—for he never had been brought up to any profession, not having the steadiness of application to make labour a pleasure; in a word, he was one of those interesting individuals whose idleness enables his Mephistophelic Majesty to make a strong bid for the fee–simple of their soul.

Archibald Smollett, like most youths of good family, with whom, for lack of employment, time hangs heavy on their hands, was not above falling in love to lend a zest to the deadly *ennui* of life. Whether or no he obeyed Celia's maxim on the matter, and did so 'only to make sport withal,' is immaterial. The fact remains that, young though he was, the love–making ended in matrimony. He had been sent to Leyden to prosecute his studies—Leyden, whose University, from about 1680 to 1730, was the great finishing school of Europe, with the lustre about it conferred by such professors as Arminius, Gomarus, Grotius, Salmasius, Scaliger, and Boerhaave. From this seat of learning young Archibald Smollett returned in ill health, but strong in his conviction that it is not good for man to be alone. Principles are as empty air if not reduced to practice. Archibald, therefore, electrified both the old Commissary and his two celibate brothers by announcing, not his intention to marry Barbara, the daughter of Mr. George Cunningham of Gilbertfield, in the county of Lanark, but the fact of its already having taken place. Probably, had the event been still in prospect, the stern old judge would have found means to check the course of true love on the score of his son's feeble health. Sir James had read his *Utopia* to some purpose, and was a stickler for legal penalties being attached to the union of persons of weak constitution. But there are limits to the intervention of even a choleric Commissary, and not all his indignation could put asunder what the Church had joined.

Passing wroth was the old man, doubtless, and tradition reports that he considered carefully the alternatives—whether to cut off his amorously inclined son with the proverbial shilling, and thereby set all the gossips' tongues in the district a–wagging over man's inhumanity to man, and that man a son, or to give him his blessing, along with a small allowance, and thus keep the name of Smollett from becoming a byword of reproach.

To induce him to adopt the latter alternative there were such reasons as these: That Miss Barbara was a young lady of great beauty and accomplishments— the Commissary had a weakness for a pretty face; that her family was as old as the Smolletts, though, having fallen upon evil days, it was not so influential; and finally, that the two families had already intermarried about a century before, when the Cunninghams, by the way, had been the more powerful of the two. The old Commissary, therefore, gave the newly–wedded pair his blessing, probably considering it better policy to bless than to ban what had already been done. On the young pair he settled an annual allowance, amounting, according to the present–day purchasing powers, to £250, as well as the liferent of the farmhouse and lands of Dalquharn, on the banks of the Leven, immediately adjoining the Bonhill estate. Well done, old Commissary, thou wast wise in thy generation. To this day the district speaks of 'Good Sir James.'

But Sir James Smollett, if he imagined he had fulfilled all the duties incumbent on him in the circumstances, and might thereafter forget the existence of the inconvenient rolling stone, received a rude awakening. The stone in question accomplished its last revolution by rolling out of existence; in other words, Archibald Smollett died in 1721, having only survived his marriage five years. He left a widow with three young children, James, Jane, and Tobias, wholly dependent on their grandfather's bounty.

Of the cant of Puritanic Presbyterianism, of its gloomy severity, of the frowns it casts on all harmless pursuits, we hear a great deal in these days of cheap criticism and a ubiquitous press. That may be all very true. There is, however, one thing in which the type never fails. Once convince it of the binding nature of any social obligations, and not all the desires of self, or the weaknesses of human nature, will be allowed to stand in the way of its fulfilment. In such crucifixion of self–interest there is conspicuous moral heroism. Of a type of nature such as this was Sir James Smollett. With a sort of cynical sneer, that if he were in for a penny he might as well be in for a pound, the old gentleman continued the allowance to the young widow's household, though on a slightly reduced scale. Dalquharn, however, was still to be the widow's home, with liberty to make as much as she could out of the farm. As she was a shrewd, capable woman, who knew the full value of a shilling, and to whom the gospel of hard work was a living creed more than a century before Thomas Carlyle preached it, the chances were all in favour of her doing well. Nay, as the sequel proved, she did better without her husband than with him, and speedily became, comparatively speaking, a 'well–to–do woman,' as the Scots phrase has it.

It was this unquestioning obedience to those provisions of the Mosaic law, 'Ye shall not afflict any widow or fatherless child: if thou afflict them in any wise, and they cry at all unto Me, I will surely hear their cry,' in which the old Commissary was a firm believer, that rendered the position of the widow and her fatherless children as secure as though they had been protected by as many deeds and settlements as would have filled a muniment room. The consequence was that, until she was no longer able to look after the farm, that is, up to the time when Smollett was preparing to go to London, Mrs. Archibald Smollett retained undisturbed possession of Dalquharn. She then went to live with her daughter, who had married Mr. Telfer, a lessee of some of the mines at Wanlockhead, and also proprietor of the estates of Scotston in Peeblesshire and Symington in Lanarkshire. The old Commissary, Sir James, was succeeded by his own son James, and then by his son George's eldest child, also called James, neither of whom left any issue. Singularly enough, the present holders of the estates are the descendants of Archibald Smollett and Barbara Cunningham; the other branches of the house having become extinct. But by neither Sir James's son nor by his grandson was Mrs. Archibald's allowance reduced.

Into this matter I have gone rather more fully than is warranted by the space at my command. But I was anxious to clear the memory of Sir James Smollett from an undeserved slur that has been cast on it by some biographers, who have been smitten with the mania for reading the facts of a man's life into his works. In Smollett's case, the opening chapters of *Roderick Random*, and the character of 'The Judge' in particular, have been assumed, on evidence the most slender, as conveying a true picture of the novelist's early relations to his grandfather and uncles. But the statement, as express as it is explicit, by Smollett himself shortly before his death, that the scenes were written under a mistaken sense of wrong, and purposely over–coloured from motives of pique and resentment that had no foundation in fact, proves that young Smollett cherished mistaken ideas of his own importance, a failing from which he suffered all his life, in imagining slights where none were intended.

The childhood and early boyhood of the youthful Tobias would not, therefore, be unhappy. Youth always looks at the sunny side of things. If his fare were plain and coarse, it was at least plentiful; if his attire were of the humblest, it was at least sufficient to keep out the cold. At this age hope is the dearest possession, and what Allan Ramsay said of his own youth may, *mutatis mutandis*, be applied to Smollett's—

'Aft hae I wade thro' glens wi' chorking feet,
When neither plaid nor kilt could fend the weet
Yet blythely would I bang oot owre the brae,
And stend owre burns as light as ony rae,
Hoping the morn might prove a better day.'

CHAPTER II

YEARS OF EDUCATION

But after the youthful Tobias had passed those momentous years when the science of suction and the art of following his nose constituted the principal ends of existence, the Scots pride in giving children a good education wherewith to begin the world, led his mother to send him early to school. As usual in such cases, during the first two years of his intellectual seedtime he was committed to the care of a worthy dame in the neighbourhood, who fulfilled the duties so admirably described by Shenstone in his *School–mistress*—the only poem of a worthy poet that has lived—

'In every village marked with little spire
Embowered in trees and hardly known to fame,
There dwells in lowly shed and mean attire
A matron old whom we schoolmistress name.'

But from the hornbook and the mysteries of 'a b, ab,' and 't o, to,' he was presently called to proceed to the scholastic establishment of one of the most famous Scots pedagogues of the eighteenth century. John Love had the reputation of having turned out more celebrated men from his various seminaries than any other teacher of his age. In addition to Smollett, Principal Robertson, Dr. Blair, Wilkie, author of the *Epigoniad*, and many other notable scholars and literary men, were his pupils. He was successively head teacher of Dumbarton Grammar School,[1] classical master in the High School of Edinburgh, and finally rector of the Dalkeith Grammar School,—a position which, as Robert Chambers says, would not now be considered the equivalent of the one he resigned to accept it. Love was first the correspondent and defender against sundry attacks on his Latin Grammar, afterwards the antagonistic critic of the great Ruddiman,—one of the last of the mighty Scots polymaths, before the days of specialists and the extension of the boundaries of learning rendered omniscience, in a humanist sense, an impossibility.

From Love the youthful Smollett received a thorough grounding in the classics, particularly in Latin. The days had not dawned when that human instrument of youthful torture known as 'the crammer' had come on the scene. Education, if conducted on wrong principles in many cases, was, at least, rational in the end it proposed to accomplish. Boys in the eighteenth century were not treated like prize turkeys, and stuffed to repletion with all and sundry items of knowledge, whereof about one per cent. is found useful in after life. Love did not believe in taking passing sips from the cup of every classic author, and then relegating their works to the dust and the spiders. His was not the system to make a sort of fox–hunt scamper over Latin literature, from Nepos to Statius, or in Greek, from Homer to Lucian, clearing difficulties at a bound, and cutting the Gordian knot of vexed passages by the rough and ready method of omission. His pupils were the *'homines unius libri'*—the men of the single book, who are always to be feared. The consequence was that to the end of life Smollett acknowledged his indebtedness to Love. He took an interest in the lad's progress, and, knowing the circumstances of his lot, and how much depended on his proficiency in the subjects of study, he paid every attention to him, and spared no pains to make him a thoroughly sound if not a very profound classical scholar. All through the long and laborious life of Smollett, the lessons of Love bore fruit.

Here, however, I must once more enter a protest against the ready credulity of several previous biographers, in believing the foul slander,—manufactured by some one utterly unacquainted with the true facts of the case,—that the portrait of the pedagogue in *Roderick Random* could possibly be intended to represent Love. Disproof the most convincing is to be found in the fact that the distinguishing characteristic of the pedagogue in the novel was his resemblance to Horace's *plagosus Orbilius*—the flogging Orbilius. But of Love's system the glory—and glory it certainly was—consisted in the total abolition of the degrading corporal punishment, in his successive schools, at the time when the sparing of the rod by any pedagogue was esteemed to be unquestionably equivalent to spoiling the child.

As to the estimation in which the youthful Smollett was held by his companions, there is but scant evidence. He seems, like many another youth, whom the stirrings of great imaginings within were beginning to puzzle and in some degree to annoy, as being unlike anything his companions experienced, to have been masterful, irritable, and proud. He even appears, with a lad's lack of judgment, to have exhibited the snobbery of family pride, that most ignoble form of vulgarity. All through life Smollett betrayed a smack of this failing—a trait of character which, long years after, led him to surround himself with his poor and needy brethren in literature, to whom he played the part of 'the Great Cham' of the press.

Mr. Robert Chambers, in his excellent biography of Smollett, in many respects still one of the best accounts of the great novelist's life and works, regards the influence of the surrounding scenery as being the main factor in turning Smollett's ideas towards imaginative and romantic themes. To a certain extent, as we have already pointed out, the charms of the district must have produced a deep impression on him. The vividness of his recollections of them in after years, and the terms of passionate delight wherewith he spoke of them, all go to prove this. But there was another agency at work.

The charms of our immortal English literature were slowly but surely casting their glamour over him. From the study of classics he had passed to that of Milton, Dryden, and of the Restoration drama, with close attention paid to that great period which had closed but a few years before his birth—the reign of Queen Anne. Chambers also states that 'Smollett, like Burns, was at a very early period struck with admiration of the character of Wallace, whose adventures, reduced from the verse of Blind Harry by Hamilton of Gilbertfield, were in every boy's hand, and formed a constant theme of fireside and nursery stories. To such a degree arose Smollett's enthusiasm on this subject, that, ere he had quitted Dumbarton School, he wrote verses to the memory of the Scottish champion.'

But schooldays could not last for ever. Besides, the young Tobias ere long lost interest in the Dumbarton Grammar School. John Love had been translated to Edinburgh, and a new pedagogue had arisen who knew not Tobias. Accordingly, the lad began to plague his mother to allow him to become a soldier like his elder brother James. The matter, of course, had to be referred to the family dictator—the old Commissary. But that stern incarnation of Puritanic duty decided that while the family interest might procure the advancement of one soldier, two were beyond its exercise of patronage. Hence he insisted on Tobias being sent to Glasgow University, to prepare for one of the learned professions, offering to bear a share in the expense of his education. But as the old man died almost immediately afterwards, namely, in 1733, before the youth was actually sent to college, the latter benefited little from his grandfather's intentions, because in his will no provision was made for the children of his youngest son. But his uncle James appears to have proved more kind–hearted than was anticipated, and to have assisted him, at least during the first years of his course.

During his attendance on the Arts classes in Glasgow University,—only one of which seems to have made any deep impression on him, namely, the lectures of Francis Hutcheson, Professor of Moral Philosophy, and father of Scots Philosophy,—he made the acquaintance of several medical students, who were then going through their curriculum, with a view to graduation in medicine. As in the case of Sir James Y. Simpson[2] it was the fact of lodging in the same house with two medical students from Bathgate, to wit, Drs. Reid and M'Arthur, which gave him the bias towards medicine that was to make the world so much his debtor, so in Smollett's case his association with these youths directed his thoughts also towards the prosecution of medicine as a career in life. In those days the difficulties of carrying out such an intention were not so great as now. Medicos were not then as plentiful as leaves in Vallombrosa, so much so that the great degree–granting institutions must for their own protection make the examinations increasingly severe, in order that the survival only of the scientifically fittest may in time relieve the congestion.

When, therefore, Smollett announced his intention to his mother and his uncle James (who only recently had succeeded to the family honours), they appeared to consider that the proposal was one to which they could give a cordial assent, although surgery had not yet commenced the wonderful march of progress achieved by it later on in the same century, and though the prestige of the craft, sadly tarnished by its association with the trade of the barber and of the phlebotomist, was by no means one calculated as yet to render its members proud of their connection with it—in Scotland at least. The genius of the three Alexander Monroes,—grandfather, father, and son, who consecutively held the chair of Anatomy in Edinburgh University for a hundred and twenty–six years, namely, from 1720 to 1846,—of Gregory, of Cullen, and of other illustrious knights of the knife, was needed to efface the lingering associations of the razor and basin, and to crown the name of surgeon with undying laurels.

This, then, was the career which Tobias George Smollett marked out for himself, hoping in the course of time, by hard work and assiduity, to obtain a position, first as surgeon's mate and afterwards as surgeon, in the navy. Only qualified surgeons were accepted by the Admiralty, and the prospect stimulated him to put forth all his exertions to qualify for the post. The friends in the Vale of Leven amongst them managed to provide the necessary funds. Tobias, in addition, was also apprenticed to a worthy man, Mr. John Gordon, who, in the quaint old Trongate of Glasgow, during the fourth, fifth, and sixth decades of the eighteenth century, discharged the dual vocations of medical practitioner and apothecary. Smollett's meagre salary or wage, eked out by what his mother and the Bonhill folks could furnish, was made to serve the purpose of paying his way through the medical classes in the University and of supplying himself with clothing. Mr. Gordon, his master, gave him a room in his house, and a cover was always laid for him at the good old surgeon's table.

A striking insight is thus afforded into the proud, irritable nature of the youth, whom poverty, in place of teaching lessons of patience and gratitude to the kindly hearts that were smoothing his life's path for him, rather stung into angry repining against such indebtedness, as well as into emphatic asseveration of their action being no more than what was due to him. Humility was at no time one of the virtues in which Smollett excelled. His *amour–propre* was of so sensitive a composition that the least breath of contradiction made, so to speak,

'Each particular hair to stand an–end,
Like quills upon the fretful porpentine.'

That Smollett studied hard during these years, that, moreover, he took every means lying within his power to increase his fund of general knowledge, as well as to amass stores of that information which lay in the line of his own special studies in medicine and science, has been recorded for us by some of his early companions. Neither a laggard nor a dullard in his work was he, as is evinced by the fact that he was devoting attention to Latin, Greek, and philosophy at the same time that he was endeavouring to master anatomy and medicine. How he was able to accomplish the achievement of acquiring even a superficial acquaintance with the subjects named, at the identical period that he was serving in his master's shop from eight in the morning till nine at night, is a mystery. Strong evidence is it of his zeal in the pursuit of knowledge, that he cheerfully prosecuted labours so onerous and so prolonged at a time when his age, according to the most liberal scale of calculation, could not have exceeded from fifteen to seventeen years. But through the gates of knowledge he already saw a means of escape for himself from the grinding penury wherein it was his lot to be cast.

John Gordon, surgeon and apothecary, to whom so beautiful a tribute is paid in *Humphrey Clinker*, appears to have shown the youthful Tobias substantial kindness. A sincere affection, on his side at least, existed towards Smollett. The latter, however, seems to have made him somewhat of a poor return for his benevolent disposition towards him, though really it is questionable whether Smollett was responsible for his frigid temperament, which showed no interest in anyone whose goodwill would not in some way react advantageously on himself. Notwithstanding that Gordon aided Smollett both by precept and purse during his years of study, the latter was in the habit of satirising him behind his back in juvenile pasquinades. The same evil spirit of social Ishmaelitism, the feeling that the world had been hard on him, and that he was therefore justified by satire and sneers in 'taking it out' of anyone else who might have relations with him, was present with him until a year or two of his death. Shortly before the great end came, this vitriolic acidulousness, as well as the saturnine bitterness of his nature, became somewhat softened. He then wrote in *Humphrey Clinker*, under the character of 'Matthew Bramble,' as follows:—'I was introduced to Mr. Gordon, a patriot of a truly noble spirit, who is father of the linen manufactory in that place, and was the great promoter of the city workhouse, infirmary, and other works of public utility. Had he lived in ancient Rome, he would have been honoured with a statue at the public expense.' Thus he made the *amende honorable*, but the description in the first instance of Gordon as 'Potion' in *Roderick Random* was cruelly unjust, though Smollett in later years declared the portraits of both 'Crab' and 'Potion' to be imaginary. In early years such was the 'sheer cussedness' of his disposition, that even at the risk of offending his dearest friends, he could not refrain from firing off some of his satirical pasquinades. In fact, until the offending devil was whipped out of him by the lash of John Wilkes' stronger controversial pen, Smollett was too ready to indulge in satirical outbursts against friend and foe alike, where his fancied infallibility chanced to be impugned.

Dr. John Gordon seemed to have had some dim, undefinable consciousness that his proud, irritable, unmanageable apprentice was destined yet to do something in the world of worthy work. Sir Walter Scott, in his *Lives of the Novelists*, remarks: 'His master expressed his conviction of Smollett's future eminence in very homely but expressive terms, when some of his neighbours were boasting the superior decorum and propriety of the pupils they possessed. "It may be all very true," said the keen–sighted Mr. Gordon; "but give me before them all my own bubbly–nosed callant with the stane in his pouch."' And Scott adds that, without attempting to render the above into English, Southern readers ought to be informed that the words contain a faithful sketch of a negligent, unlucky, but spirited urchin, never without some mischievous prank in his head, and a stone in his pocket ready to execute it. Better portrait than this of the young Tobias could not be desired. Only one other boyish trait shall we add to illustrate his readiness of resource in extricating himself and others from awkward predicaments. From Dr. Moore's *Life of Smollett* we take it—a volume upon which all succeeding biographers have had to draw, as he had the privilege of personal intercourse with the novelist. 'On a winter evening, when the streets were covered with snow, Smollett happened to be engaged in a snowball fight with a few boys of his own age. Among his associates was the apprentice of that surgeon who is supposed to have been delineated under the name of "Crab" in *Roderick Random*. He entered his shop while his apprentice was in the heat of the engagement. On the return of the latter, the master remonstrated with him severely for his negligence in quitting the shop. The youth excused himself by saying, that while he was employed in making up a prescription, a fellow hit him with a snowball in the teeth, and that he had been in pursuit of the delinquent. "A mighty probable story, truly," said the master in an ironical tone. "I wonder how long I should stand here," added he, "before it would enter into mortal man's head to throw a snowball at me." While he was holding his head erect with a most scornful air, he received a very severe blow in the face by a snowball. Smollett, who stood concealed behind the pillar at the shop door, had heard the dialogue, and, perceiving that his companion was puzzled for an answer, he extricated him by a repartee equally smart and *àpropos*.'

But it must not be supposed, pardonable though it might be, considering his early love of rollicking fun, that all his spare time was spent in roistering horseplay like the above. Such an incident as it must assuredly be relegated to the early days of apprenticeship. Meagre though the facts are which have descended to us of his residence in Glasgow, that he studied both hard and perseveringly is proved by the position he secured in his final medical examination. Not for a moment do I desire to institute any comparison between the standard or extent of requirements demanded in order to qualify for a medical degree nowadays, and that which gave Smollett his first step on the medical ladder. In those days physicians were in reality supervised by no competent board as to their qualifications, and surgeons, despite the navy regulations, were in a case very little better. At the same time, to accept the description Smollett gives in *Roderick Random* of the 'first and only' professional examination candidates were expected to undergo prior to obtaining an appointment in the service, would be uncharitable. The creator of *Roderick Random* was still in his youthfully exuberant period, when fidelity to fact was esteemed by him as a very secondary consideration, provided a piquant, sarcastic colouring was imparted to the incidents. Not until he became a historian did Smollett really learn, in a literary sense, to recognise the value of truthfulness in delineation.

From the records of Glasgow University for 1738–39, the facts are to be gleaned that he passed with approbation his examination in anatomy and medicine, and was thereafter qualified to practise as a surgeon. But whether comprehensive or not as a course of medical study, the curriculum was sufficient to endow him with a knowledge of his profession, quite adequate for all the professional calls afterwards made on it. From the unconscious testimony of his own works, in the number and accuracy of the medical references contained therein, we are able to gauge the range and depth of his surgical and scientific knowledge. For the times wherein he lived, his acquaintance with matters the most recondite was extraordinary.

Not only, however, had his studies been of a scientifico–medical character. English literature in more than one of its manifold departments was made the subject of systematic reading. To the plays of Otway, Davenant, Dryden, Rowe, Southerne, and other post–Revolution tragedy writers, he devoted close attention. To the romantic tales of French literature, and to their imitations by Robert Greene, Mrs. Aphra Behn, Mrs. Manley, and others, he likewise turned with delight, while we learn from his own correspondence at this period that he drank deep draughts of Milton, Cowley, and Dryden, whose earlier poems he especially admired. The fruit of these studies appeared in a tragedy entitled *The Regicide*, written during the last year of his University work. Dealing with an outstanding event in early Scottish history, an event that afforded scope for considerable diversity of opinion as to the nobility or otherwise of the motives actuating the murderers of James I., the drama could have been made a great psychological and ethical study in the hands of a stronger writer. But as Smollett was neither a Cowley nor a Milton, able to produce verse at thirteen and sixteen worthy to be compared with the work of men twenty years their seniors, *The Regicide* is but a sorry production. A curious problem how far a man is fitted to act as his own critic is raised by

The Regicide. Nine readers out of every ten who peruse the work will toss it on one side contemptuously as the immature ravings of a callow poet. Yet, until he had been five years editor of the *Critical Review*,—that *olla podrida* of everything that was not criticism, along with a great deal that was of the best type of it,—he believed almost as implicitly as in his own salvation, that *The Regicide* was not much less notable a play than any of Shakespeare's, but had been sacrificed by the spleen of envious rivals and knavish managers. But the point settled by it at this stage of our inquiry is that young Tobias had not idled his time during his University days. Not only had he taken a good place in the estimation of his examiners, but the fruit of the occupation of his spare time is a tragedy, for a youth of nineteen a sufficiently notable achievement, though not by any means so when we regard it as the mature expression of manhood's ideas, as Smollett later on asserted it to be. In 1738–9, Smollett completed his studies, passed his examination, and then faced the future manfully, to see what indications of weal or of woe it might hold for him.

CHAPTER III

WANDERJAHRE

Smollett's *Lehrjahre* were over, his *Wanderjahre* were about to commence. After passing his examination in Glasgow, he returned for a time to his mother's house at Dalquharn, glad once more to feel himself among the scenes of his early boyhood. Changes great and manifold had, however, taken place there. His grandfather had, as we have seen, died some years before, so had his uncle, James Smollett; and now another James, the son of the old Commissary's second son, George, and therefore a full cousin of Tobias, was laird of Bonhill. His mother, though still undisturbed in her tenancy of Dalquharn, was preparing to spend at least one half of each year with her daughter Jane, Smollett's only sister, who had a month or two before been married to Mr. Telfer. Home was no longer home to him. His eldest brother was away with his regiment, the friends of boyhood's years were either scattered or had formed new ties. He felt, as he said in one of his letters, 'like a bird that returns to find its nest torn down and harried.'

For him in his new profession there was of course no opening in his native district. The thriving village of Renton did not come into existence until 1782, eleven years after Smollett's death. Dumbarton also was well supplied with medical practitioners; therefore his only chance lay in going farther afield. His mother would have liked to keep her Benjamin near her, but Benjamin had all the prodigal son's love of roving without his vices. Besides, his studies in English literature had inflamed him with the desire to throw himself into the great literary gladiatorial arena—London. His friends were overborne by his enthusiasm. He was brimming over with all youth's sanguine hopes. He would succeed, in fact, he could not fail to succeed, was his insistent assurance. Alas! he had yet to learn in the hard school of disappointment that in nine cases out of ten the battle is not to the strong, nor the race to the swift, but that literary success then as now was a lottery, wherein the least worthy often bears away the prize.

The days were past when the head of the family, the laird of Bonhill, could afford material assistance to any youthful scion of the house proceeding out into the battle of life. Beyond good wishes and a bulky sheaf of introductions, his cousin, James Smollett, had little to give Tobias. As it was, however, the future novelist carried away from his native place the best of all recommendations and heritages, an unsullied character, with an indomitable love of honest independence that atones for a multitude of less lovely traits. 'What kind of work you individually can do ... the first of all problems for a man to find out, that is the thing a man is born to in all epochs,' were the wise and weighty words of Thomas Carlyle in his Rectorial address. To

Tobias Smollett the problem in question was one whereto he applied himself with all youth's jaunty assurance. At nineteen the point at issue usually is not 'What career am I fit for?' but 'What career shall I choose?' a faculty, a capacity for all being confidently presupposed as a precedent certainty. Youth can make no calculation of probabilities. The ratios of chance are always esteemed likely to favour the young gladiator. So with Smollett. With a light heart he went forth to the deadly battle of life, recking not that the Goliath of failure and disappointment was waiting for him almost at the parting of the ways, and that the only pebbles in his bag were a boyish tragedy, and the certificate of surgical proficiency from an obscure Scottish medical school. With such weapons, would he prove successful in the impending strife? From this second point of view the aphorism is once more apposite, that the battle is not to the strong.

In 1740, therefore, Tobias Smollett took farewell of his Dumbartonshire home, and turned his face Londonwards—one more tiny unit to be sucked down for a time into the moiling, whirling, indistinguishable crowd revolving in the vortex of the mighty social maelstrom. Fearlessly as Schiller's 'Diver' did the youth plunge into 'the howling Charybdis below'; but, alas! the effects of the sufferings, both mental and physical, which he underwent ere 'he rose to the surface again,' were to follow hard on his footsteps, even to the end of life. Even as Thomas de Quincey, sixty years after, was to find Oxford Street a stony–hearted stepmother, so Smollett, alone in the mighty metropolis, was made to realise, with an insistence that burned itself into his inmost heart, that no solitary in the Sahara is more isolated than he who is, unknowing and unknown, an atom in a vast London crowd. Men in after years talked glibly of the irritability of the great novelist. They could not realise in their shallow complacency what a crucifixion those years of failure were to the proud, unbending spirit. Had Smollett been less self–confident, he would have suffered less. To a mind like his, it was the crushing consciousness of a mistaken estimate of his own powers that infused into his nature that strain of gall that manifests itself even in the brightest of his writings.

To London therefore Smollett repaired with high hopes. That these were based upon his tragedy rather than on his medical acquirements is evident from his letters of this period, as well as from the preface to *The Regicide*, when, later on, it was published. Like another Scot, who nine years afterwards was to 'hasten' to London with his tragedy of *Agis*, only to meet with like mortification, to wit, John Home, Smollett imagined he had only to present his play to the managers of the leading theatres to secure its instant acceptance. He was roughly disillusionised. In the first place, the merits of *The Regicide* are of the scantiest. Its boyishness and immaturity, its stiffness and bombast, are perceptible on every page. The characters, again, are perpetually firing off such exclamations and expletives as, 'Tremendous powers!' 'O fatal chance!' 'Mysterious fate!' 'Infernal homicide!' and the like, scarce a speech being ungarnished by one of them. No sooner had Smollett arrived in London than he hastened to lay his tragedy before the managers of the theatres. After prolonged delays it was returned to him declined. Though his vanity was cut to the quick by this neglect of his genius, as he considered it, he looked so far to the main chance that he endeavoured to induce Lord Lyttleton to use his interest with Mr. Rich, Mr. Garrick, or Mr. Lacy, the great theatrical managers of the day. The only particular wherein that nobleman seems to have been blameworthy was that, out of excess of amiability, he did not care to wound the author's feelings by telling him of the lack of merit in his play. Smollett, however, accused him and the managers, along with his other patrons, of well–nigh all the crimes under heaven, because of their failure to perceive in his tragedy beauties that had no place there. To resurrect the whole controversy would be as unprofitable as to retail one of last century's stale jokes. Those who desire to pursue the investigation will find the circumstances recounted by Smollett in his silly preface to *The Regicide*, when, some years subsequent, he published it by subscription—that is, after the success of *Roderick Random* had rendered him famous. He was weak enough, also, to endeavour to satirise the parties to his disappointment in the novel in question. The story of Melopoyn and his attempt to obtain recognition of his dramatic genius is, *mutatis mutandis*, intended to represent Smollett's own case.

The small store of guineas which the youth had brought with him from Scotland were meantime fast vanishing. Any remunerative employment seemed as far distant as ever. The prejudice in London against impecunious Scots was then at its height. All very well was it for such men as Arbuthnot, Thomson, Mallet, and Mickle to speak of the favour shown them in London by King, Court, and Government. Against these four, who were wafted into the haven of popularity by propitious gales almost at the very outset of their literary career, how many scores are there, little inferior to them in genius, as well as learning, who sank into Grub Street hacks through not having any patron to recommend their productions? The patronless man was a pariah, even as in feudal days a villein without a lord was ranked as a wild beast.

Although the narrative in *Roderick Random* of the hero's treatment at the Navy Office, the examination he passed, the means whereby he was enabled in the end to get appointed as surgeon's assistant, are exaggerated, still there must have been a solid substratum of fact drawn from the author's own experience in similar circumstances. Regarding this period of Smollett's life the information is exceedingly meagre. That he went through terrible privations, can be guessed from the fact that he informed John Home he shuddered whenever he remembered those days. How he obtained a position on board the *Cumberland*, an eighty–gun vessel in the fleet commanded by Sir Challoner Ogle, there is now no means of ascertaining. Whether through the pressgang, like Roderick Random, or by some other channel more legitimate and honourable, is unknown. Mr. David Hannay, in his admirable and valuable life of Smollett, states that there is no certainty which of the sixteen ships in Ogle's fleet he served on. Dr. Anderson, in his life of the novelist, relates that Smollett left his name carved on the timbers of the *Cumberland*. But an examination of her books reveals no such name as *Smollett*, though a *Smalley* does occur, and the shadow of a probability is thereby raised that a mistake in names may have been made.

Be this as it may, one fact is certain,—Smollett was present at the expedition to Carthagena, whatever might be the ship in which he sailed, and whatsoever the capacity wherein he served. On this point Carlyle's statements in *Frederick the Great* (to be cited further on), though pronounced by some critics only another example of Carlylean exaggeration, are by no means wide of the mark. The expedition to Carthagena was one of the most gigantic crimes ever perpetrated by a Government, while its mismanagement is an ineffaceable blot on the British army and navy. Spain had looked with a jealous eye upon the progress of the British American colonies. All that lay in her power she did to harass them. British commerce was suffering, but the Ministry of Sir Robert Walpole seemed utterly indifferent to the prestige of the national arms, or even to the safety of the colonial possessions. As Smollett long years afterwards stated in his *History of England*, 'no effectual attempt had been made to annoy the enemy. Expensive squadrons had been equipped, had made excursions, and had returned without striking a blow. Admiral Vernon had written from the West Indies to his private friends that he was neglected and in danger of being sacrificed. Notwithstanding the numerous navy of Great Britain, Spanish privateers made prizes of the British merchant ships with impunity.' A complete paralysis seemed to have fallen on the national energies, consequent on the *laissez-faire* policy of the peace–loving Whig Premier, Sir Robert Walpole. At last the exasperation of the nation, with the disgraces that had fallen upon it, both in Europe and South America, burst all bounds, and swept Minister and Government along with the popular enthusiasm.

As Jamaica had long been threatened by certain Spanish ships of war with land forces on board, Sir Challoner Ogle was ordered to proceed with his vessels thither to effect a junction with Admiral Vernon. Accordingly, the fleet, of which the *Cumberland* was one, set sail in November, and reached Jamaica on the 9th January 1741. Vernon now found himself at the head of the most formidable naval force that had ever visited those seas, while the land forces were also strong in proportion. Had this armament been ready to act under the command of wise and experienced commanders, united in counsels and steadily attached to the honour and interests of their country, the whole of Spain's possessions in the Western Hemisphere would now have belonged to Britain. But, owing to the death of Lord Cathcart, the general in command of the land forces, the command devolved on General Wentworth, a man utterly unfit for the position. Admiral Vernon (also a nincompoop) and he spent their time and energies in counteracting each other's influence, and actually taking steps to frustrate each other's plans. Finding that the Spanish admiral, De Torres, had retired from Jamaica, in place of following him to Havannah, Vernon decided to attack Carthagena, and sailed thither, despite Wentworth's remonstrances. This was blunder No. 1. The second was in attempting to prosecute the enterprise in the face of such divided counsels. The consequence was a terrible loss of life by disease and the risks of war, because neither commander seemed to care how many were killed, provided they were not his own men. Therefore neither supported the other. The horrors of that expedition are past belief. Smollett's grim and ghastly picture of them, in his 'Account of the Expedition against Carthagena,' in the *Compendium of Voyages and Travels*, and in *Roderick Random*, is not over–coloured. We shall note it in its place, but meantime let us see what Carlyle has now to say to the case. In chapter xii. of *Frederick the Great*, under the heading 'Sorrows of Britannic Majesty,' he writes of the Carthagena expedition: 'Most obscure among the other items in that Armada of Sir Challoner's just taking leave of England; most obscure of the items then, but now most noticeable or almost alone noticeable, is a young surgeon's mate—one Tobias Smollett, looking over the waters there and the fading coasts, not without thoughts. A proud, soft–hearted, though somewhat stern–visaged, caustic, and indignant young gentleman; apt to be caustic in speech, having sorrows of his own under lock and key, on this and subsequent occasions. Excellent Tobias, he has, little as he hopes it, something considerable by way of mission in this expedition and in this universe generally. Mission to take portraiture of English seamen, with the due grimness, due fidelity, and convey the same to remote generations before it vanish. Courage, my brave young Tobias, through endless sorrows, contradictions, toils, and confusions. You will do your errand in some measure, and that will be something.'

To describe in detail the hideous drama of mismanagement and sacrifice of valuable lives that ensued in consequence of Wentworth's incapacity, and of the strained relations between him and Admiral Vernon, would be out of place here. Suffice it to say that, though British valour, in spite of adverse circumstances, gained one or two successes, the expedition as a whole was a ghastly failure. Let us instead exhibit the awful picture Smollett afterwards drew of the condition of things immediately prior to the breaking up of the siege—a picture that thrilled England with horror, and led eventually, along with one or two other contributory circumstances, to the complete reorganisation of the naval service of the country. In addition, it blasted for ever, and deservedly so, the careers of monsters so inhuman as Wentworth and Vernon. 'As for the sick and wounded,' says Smollett, 'they were next day sent on board of the transports and vessels called hospital ships, where they languished in want of every necessary comfort and accommodation. They were destitute of surgeons, nurses, cooks, and proper provision; they were pent up between decks in small vessels, where they had not room to sit upright; they wallowed in filth; myriads of maggots were hatched in the putrefaction of their sores, which had no other dressing than that of being washed by themselves with their own allowance of brandy; and nothing was heard but groans, lamentations, and the language of despair, invoking death to deliver them from their miseries. What served to encourage this despondence was the prospect of those poor wretches who had the strength and opportunity to look about them. For there they beheld the naked bodies of their fellow–soldiers and comrades floating up and down the harbour, affording prey to the carrion crows and sharks, which tore them in pieces without interruption, and contributing by their stench to the mortality that prevailed. The picture cannot fail to be shocking to the humane reader, especially while he is informed that while these miserable objects cried in vain for assistance, and actually perished for want of proper attendance, every ship of war in the fleet could have spared a couple of surgeons for their relief; and many young gentlemen of that profession solicited their captains in vain for leave to go and administer help to the sick and wounded; but the discord between the chiefs was inflamed to such a degree of diabolical rancour, that the one chose rather to see his men perish than ask help of the other, who disdained to offer his assistance unasked, though it might have saved the lives of his fellow–subjects.'

Such, then, was the frightful fiasco of the Carthagena expedition, in which the young Tobias served, and, by his serving as a humble surgeon's mate, was able to render a service to his country, the beneficial effects of which are felt to this day. Not only did he expose the awful consequences of personal animosity between the leaders of a great naval–military expedition. Great as was that service, the second was greater still. David Hannay felicitously remarks: 'It was Smollett's good fortune that he saw the navy at the very lowest ebb it has reached since there was a navy in England. In 1740 it was as little organised as it had been in the seventeenth century. There was more flogging and more callous cruelty in every way than there had been a century earlier.' A truer statement of fact could scarcely be made. The navy at that period was suffering in common with the army from the disastrous effects of the Whig Walpole's peace–at–any–price policy. In fact, there was no proper Admiralty supervision by permanent officials. Everything was at the mercy of party scheming and intrigue. Incompetency ruled in all departments. Not until the accession of the elder Pitt was there a change for the better. British prestige was dragged through the mire of disgrace in every corner of the world, and the affairs of the navy were simply left to direct themselves, while the individuals nominally in charge squabbled and plotted for place and power.

It was by his immortal pictures in *Roderick Random* and *Peregrine Pickle* of the horrors of navy service, and of the ignorance and brutality characterising the men who were proudly termed 'the tars of Old England,' that Smollett really revolutionised the navy. Slow though the improvements might be in filtering through the various strata of the service, from Admiralty to seamen, the first note of reform was struck when Smollett penned that awfully realistic picture of life on board the *Thunder* man–of–war, with the characters of Captain Oakum, Surgeon MacShane, and the others connected with that floating hell. In our concluding chapters we shall examine the truthfulness or otherwise of Smollett's character–painting. Here, however, it may be remarked that the description of the facts, as well as the local 'atmosphere,' have been reported by those present at the attack on Carthagena, and serving in the navy at the time, to be absolutely correct.

After the failure of the expedition, the shattered and disgraced fleet betook itself to Jamaica to refit. While here, Smollett decided that he had seen enough of navy life, and that henceforth his labours would lie ashore. The beauty of the island tempted him to settle there. Accordingly, he retired from the service after fifteen months' experience of it, and started practice as a doctor in the island. What his success was cannot now be ascertained. In less than two years he is found in London, namely, in the beginning of 1744, striving once more to gain a living in the great metropolis.

Only one influence followed him into life from the sunny island of Jamaica. He there wooed and won Miss Anne or Nancy Lascelles, a young Kingston heiress. When he returned to London, he returned as an engaged man. In one of his unpublished letters, he expressly states that he was not married until 1747, when Miss Lascelles came to England. But, on the other hand, there is evidence in Jamaica that some sort of ceremony was performed before Smollett left the island in the end of 1743. However this may be, Smollett's *Wanderjahre* or years of wandering were now over. He settled down straightway to do the work Heaven laid to his hand, with all the energy that in him lay.

CHAPTER IV

THE WEARY TRAGEDY—SHIFTS TO LIVE

No sooner had Smollett returned to London than he resumed negotiations with reference to his ill–fated tragedy. Authors are proverbially blind to the true merits of their literary progeny. As each fond father's geese are swans, so, in the youthful Tobias Smollett's eyes, fresh from conquest in the matrimonial arena, this decided objection to have anything to do with his play could only result from national antipathy against the Scots. 'My luckless tragedy is suffering for Bannockburn,' he remarked on one occasion to Mallet. Our vanity will seize on any reason rather than the right one to save our *amour–propre*. Undoubtedly, Rich, Gifford, and Lacy's treatment of Smollett was far from generous, nor was Garrick wholly free from blame. They should have declined the play at once. Let us take the better view of it, however, and ascribe their action to a mistaken desire to save the peppery Scotsman's feelings. Better a hundred times if he had received the plain, unvarnished truth about that wretchedly crude production at the outset. A few pangs of wounded vanity, a curse or two at the Southron's lack of critical insight, and Tobias probably would have buried or burned his MS. and forgotten all about it in another year, while in the long–run his common sense would have come to see the justice of the managerial decision. But for several years after his return from Jamaica his expectations were raised and his hopes excited by vague promises and vaguer hints as to what 'we will do next year.' The consequence of all this manœuvring was, that Tobias, with that obstinate national pride characteristic of him, conceived that in some occult way patriotic prestige was bound up in his publishing, by hook or crook, a production so long withheld from a presumably expectant public by Southron jealousy. More follies have been perpetrated under the guise of patriotism than through all the vices combined. Let us detail the finish of a foolish business. After *Roderick Random* had rendered him famous, Smollett, imagining that all he wrote or had ever written would be eagerly devoured by an undiscriminating public, published *The Regicide* by subscription. Ten years afterwards he cursed his indiscretion in no measured terms. The wisdom of thirty became the folly of forty; and some time during the last two years of his life, according to tradition, he committed to the flames two or three dozen copies of the ill–digested tragedy that had entailed on him so much trouble and brought him so little reputation.

Meantime, the worthy Tobias was oppressed with the all–absorbing problem wherewithal to live. Rumour credited him with marrying an heiress. Rumour, as usual, lied. If our ex–surgeon's mate, whose philosophy of life at that period seemed summed up in Horace's famous injunction, 'Get money, honestly if you can, but without fail get money,' expected that in marrying

Miss Nancy Lascelles he was purchasing the fee–simple of future years of affluence and ease, never man was more deceived. Let us credit the estimable Tobias, however, with a moral code more elevated than that. Albeit in the years to come Miss Nancy found she had not married a blood–relation of the patient Job's, and he, that passionate West Indian 'heiresses' are not the ideal wives for hard–working literary men, on the whole the marriage was as happy as are three out of every five contracted in this working–day world. But the fortune of Miss Nancy, being invested in sugar plantations and such accessories as are necessary for the efficient production of this necessary staple of food, was, alas! difficult of realisation, and in the end only rolled upon the already heavily–burdened husband a quiverful of lawsuits. It was the old story! The lawyers got the cash, the litigants—the unspeakable pleasure of paying for their law with the object of their law–suit. Thus did Miss Nancy's fortune disappear!

From March 1744, when he returned to London, until January 1748, when *Roderick Random* was published, Smollett's movements are involved in obscurity. Only by means of meagre references in his own letters, and chance allusions to him in those of such friends as, in days to come, having carved their names in the Temple of Fame, had, in consequence, the somewhat doubtful honour of having their lives written, are we able to glean aught about his existence at this period. He was only a lad of some three or four–and–twenty years, unknown, friendless, and left to fight the great battle of life for himself. Little wonder is it, then, if, among the half–million inhabitants constituting the population of the British metropolis about the middle of the eighteenth century, the young Scots surgeon felt himself lost— as though he had been cut off from every kindly face and sympathetic voice. He probably was beginning to form those connections with booksellers which led him, before many years were over, to degenerate into a mere money–grubbing hack, not above doing a little literary 'sweating,' by obtaining high prices for work which he got executed by his slaves of the quill on terms much lower. But of that in its place. Certain it is that during these four years Smollett must have derived an income, and, what is more, a moderately good income, from some source. His letters prove that. From one addressed to his early friend, Richard Barclay, and dated London, May 22, 1744, we quote the following autobiographical facts:—'I am this minute happy in yours, which affords me all the satisfaction of hearing from you, without the anxiety naturally flowing from its melancholy occasion, for I was informed of the decease of our late friend by a letter from Mr. Gordon, dated the day after his death. All those (as well as you, my dear Barclay) who knew the intimacy between us must imagine that no stroke of fate could make a deeper impression on my soul than that which severs me for ever from one I so entirely loved, from one who merited universal esteem, and who, had he not been cut off in the very blossom of his being, would have been an ornament to society, the pride and joy of his parents, and a most inestimable jewel to such as were attached to him as we were by the sacred ties of love and friendship.... My weeping muse would fain pay a tribute to his manes, and were I vain enough to think my verse would last, I would perpetuate his friendship and his virtue. I wish I was near you, that I might pour forth my heart before you, and make you judge of its dictates and the several steps I have lately taken, in which case I am confident you and all honest men would acquit my principles, however my prudentials might be condemned. However, I have moved into the house where the late John Douglas, surgeon, died, and you may henceforth direct for Mr. Smollett, surgeon, in Downing Street, West.... Your own,

TS. SMOLLETT.

N.B.—Willie Wood, who is just now drinking a glass with me, offers you his good wishes, and desires you to present his compliments to Miss Betty Bogle.—T. S.'

Now, the extracts given above would seem to indicate that Smollett was, in the first place, in somewhat easy circumstances. As Mr. Hannay very justly remarks, houses in Downing Street, West, and glasses of wine for friends, were not to be enjoyed, even in the patriarchal times of last century, without a periodical production of the almighty dollar. Circumstances point to the fact that Smollett took the deceased surgeon's house with the possible hope of dropping into his practice. But in addition to that very problematic source of income, there must have been some other, and that in some degree at least to be relied upon. Smollett would never have faced the future so gaily with such a millstone round his neck, unless he had clearly seen his way to a sure and steady means of revenue. To our mind, that revenue must either have been yielded by Mrs. Smollett's property in Kingston, and the ceremony performed there, prior to Smollett's departure, must have been regarded as a marriage, or his industry in hack work for the booksellers must have been phenomenal. Either alternative presents difficulties. Neither can be accepted without weighty reservations. Best, under all aspects of the case, is it to affirm nothing positively, in the absence at the present time of definite information, which, however, may yet be discovered.

The years 1745 and 1746 were stirring years in Britain. The rumours of a great Jacobite invasion of Scotland were rife while the year was young. They increased in number and definiteness as it gradually grew older, until, in August 1745, the intelligence reached London that Prince Charles Edward had actually landed in the Western Highlands. Smollett, though a sentimental Whig and an actual Tory, though, in other words, sympathising with the cause of the downtrodden and the laborious poor, while at the same time he heartily anathematised Walpole and the Duke of Newcastle, and at this time at least extolled the Tory Pitt the elder, was no Jacobite. True it was, his peppery nature was easily aroused by the flagrant and criminal neglect Scotland had received under Walpole's administration. He was never done denouncing this 'direct descendant of the impenitent thief'—a phrase afterwards borrowed, with a slight alteration, but without acknowledgment, by Dan O'Connell, and applied, as everybody knows, to Benjamin Disraeli. But however deeply Smollett was attached to his country, it was merely a sentimental attachment, akin to his Whiggery. He would not endanger his neck by 'going out' during the Rebellion of the '45, but he would have been guilty of a little harmless treason had he met with any kindred spirit with an enthusiasm strong enough to blow his own into flame. An evidence of the interest Smollett took in the Rebellion, and the indignation he felt over the atrocities perpetrated by the Duke of Cumberland on the hapless Highland prisoners that fell into his hands after the battle of Culloden, is found in the following anecdote related by Sir Walter Scott, on the authority of Robert Graham, Esq., of Gartmore, a particular friend and trustee of Smollett:— 'Some gentlemen, having met in a tavern, were amusing themselves before supper with a game at cards, while Smollett, not choosing to play, sat down to write. One of the company, who also was nominated one of his trustees (Gartmore himself), observing his earnestness, and supposing he was writing verses, asked him if it were not so. He accordingly read them the first sketch of his "Tears of Scotland," consisting only of six stanzas, and on their remarking that the termination of the poem, being too strongly expressed, might give offence to persons whose political opinions were different, he sat down without reply, and with an air of great indignation subjoined the concluding stanza:—

"While the warm blood bedews my veins,
And unimpaired remembrance reigns,
Resentment of my country's fate
Within my filial breast shall beat.
Yes, spite of thine insulting foe,
My sympathising verse shall flow.
Mourn, hapless Caledonia, mourn
Thy banished peace, thy laurels torn!"'

To which Scott adds: 'To estimate the generous emotions with which Smollett was actuated on this occasion, it must be remarked that his patriotism was independent of party feeling, as he had been bred up in Whig principles, which were those of his family. Although these appear from his historical works to have been in some degree modified, yet the author continued attached to the principles of the Revolution.'

The 'Tears of Scotland,' the poem written under the curious circumstances recounted above, was a generous outburst of patriotic indignation in favour of Scotland and the Scots, at a time when such manifestations, owing to the Jacobite Rebellion of 1745, were liable to be construed, by a Government as truculent and short–sighted as it was venal and corrupt, into treason. Notwithstanding the fact that the 'Tears of Scotland' was moderately popular in its day, the powers that were in those days decided to leave the peppery Scot severely alone.

At this period it is also that we obtain a pleasant side–light thrown upon Smollett's life and work from the autobiography of Dr. 'Jupiter' Carlyle, the minister of Inveresk, in Midlothian, from 1748 to 1805, who was the friend and associate of nearly all the literary celebrities of the period—Home, Robertson, Blair, Logan, Henry Mackenzie, Lords Kames and Monboddo, etc. Fortunately, he preserved and noted down his impressions of all these great men, though, having done so only in extreme old age, many of the details are incorrectly stated. Dr. Carlyle remarks that with Smollett and one or two more he 'resorted to a small tavern in the corner of Cockspur Street at the Golden Ball, where we had a frugal supper and a little punch, as the finances of none of the company were in very good order. But we had rich enough conversation on literary subjects, which was enlivened by Smollett's agreeable stories, which he told with a peculiar grace. Soon after our acquaintance, Smollett showed me his tragedy of "James I. of Scotland,"[3] which he never could bring on the stage. For this the managers could not be blamed, though it soured him against them, and he appealed to the public by printing it; but the public seemed to take part with the managers.'

The following incident, detailed by Dr. Carlyle, also manifests Smollett in the light of a Scots patriot:—'I was in the coffee–house with Smollett when the news of the battle of Culloden arrived, and when London all over was in an uproar of joy. It was then that Jack Stewart, the son of the Provost, behaved in the manner I before mentioned.[4] About nine o'clock I wished to go home to Lyon's in New Bond Street, as I had promised to sup with him that night, it being the anniversary of his marriage–night, or the birthday of one of his children. I asked Smollett if he was ready to go, as he lived at Mayfair; he said he was, and would conduct me. The mob were so riotous and the squibs so numerous and incessant, that we were glad to go into a narrow entry to put our wigs in our pockets, and to take our swords from our belts, and to walk with them in our hands, as everybody then wore swords; and after cautioning me against speaking a word, lest the mob should discover my country and become insolent, "for John Bull," said he, "is as haughty and valiant to–night as he was abject and cowardly on the Black Wednesday when the Highlanders were at Derby." After we got to the head of the Haymarket through incessant fire, the doctor led me by narrow lanes, where we met nobody but a few boys at a pitiful bonfire, who very civilly asked us for sixpence, which I gave them. I saw not Smollett again for some time after, when he showed Smith and me the MS. of his "Tears of Scotland," which was published not long after, and had such a run of approbation. Smollett, though a Tory, was not a Jacobite, but he had the feelings of a Scotch gentleman on the reported cruelties that were said to be exercised after the battle of Culloden.'

Sir Walter Scott, with his wonted charity, endeavours to account for Smollett's lack of success as a physician. He did not succeed, because his haughty and independent spirit neglected the bypaths which lead to fame in that profession. Another writer ascribes it to his lack of consideration for his female patients, certainly not from want of address or figure, but from a hasty impatience in listening to petty complaints. Perhaps, finally, remarks Scott, Dr. Smollett was too soon discouraged, and abandoned prematurely a profession in which success is proverbially slow.

In these circumstances, conscious as he must have been of his own powers, Smollett could only look to his pen for the supply of his daily needs. And it did not disappoint him. In 1748, besides numerous ephemeral compilations for the booksellers, he produced his poetical satire *Advice*, a poem in the manner of Juvenal, wherein several of the leading political characters of the day were held up to scorn. Our author certainly did not spare his caustic sarcasm. The consequence was, *Advice* became so popular that he published a sequel, or rather continuation of it, in 1747, under the title of *Reproof*, both being bound and published together in the succeeding year. When another edition of each was called for, Smollett had made himself talked about and feared, in the hope that the Ministry of the day would see it to their advantage to pension him off with a sinecure office. No such fortune befell him. He had only sown dragon's teeth, from which enemies sprang up to harass and vex him even to the end of his days.

Of the literary merits of the Satires more will be said anon. One quality in them may be noted here, however, and that was the absolute fearlessness wherewith Smollett attacked those in power. His sting was never sheathed out of dread of any man. None were exempt from the lash of his sarcasm, whose wrong–doings came to his knowledge. If the innocent sometimes were involved with the guilty in common condemnation, in most cases the reason was because they continued in association with the politically or morally depraved after being cognisant of their character.

The sensation created by these trenchant Satires was great. Literary London recognised that a new writer of great and varied powers had risen. The old generation was dying out. Swift, Bolingbroke, Congreve, Arbuthnot, Pope, were either dead or had ceased to write. Goldsmith had not yet appeared. Johnson alone held the field; but he was more of a moral censor than a satirist. There was really no satirist of surpassing ability tickling the palate of the public, which dearly loves censure—when directed against other people. The coarse, sledge–hammer caricature of Tom D'Urfey and Tom Brown, though still relished by a few, was gradually giving place to a more refined and incisive, but none the less vitriolic type, wherein Smollett was an acknowledged master. *Advice* and *Reproof* are readable yet for the pungency of the sarcasm, united to absolute truth as regards the facts adduced. One does not wonder at the popularity of these pieces. They are thoroughly 'live' epigrammatic productions, aglow with human interest, and palpitating with that vigorous, honest, healthy indignation against wrong which awakens a reciprocal feeling in one's breast across the chasm of a hundred and fifty years. 'Dost not fear the Government, Smollett'? said a timid friend to him after their publication. 'Fear the Government?' was the contemptuous reply of the other. 'I might if I showed I dreaded them; but no man need fear a Government provided he does not show he fears it.'

During the publication of the second part of his Satires, Smollett was joined in London by the lady who became his wife. In 1747 they set up house, and for some months he enjoyed the luxury of his own fireside. Fate was not long to leave him unassailed, but long enough, at least, to give him a taste of that hymeneal heaven which follows the union of two loving hearts—long enough for him to have experienced the sentiments that found expression in the one love–poem he wrote, 'Ode to Blue–Eyed Ann.' Miss Anne or Nancy Lascelles cannot have been the unresponsive being some of Smollett's biographers contend, in order to excuse their hero's ungallant conduct in later years, when every other sentiment was sacrificed to ambition, otherwise she could not have inspired feelings so passionate as these—

'When rolling seasons cease to change,
Inconstancy forget to range;
When lavish May no more shall bloom
Nor gardens yield a rich perfume;
When Nature from her sphere shall start,
I'll tear my Nanny from my heart.'

Smollett seemed to have all an Irishman's love of a quarrel. He never appeared happier than when he was 'slangwhanging' some unfortunate, though it is a hundred to one the fault was on his own side. To be 'slangwhanged' in return, however, was altogether another matter. Ridicule cut him to the raw. He had the idea that all the world should submit to his animadversions patiently and uncomplainingly. But if any dared to retaliate, instantly they were dubbed rogues, and fools, and blockheads. An instance of this occurred in his relations with Rich, the theatrical manager. The success of *Advice* had induced the latter to lend a favourable ear to Smollett's proposal to write the libretto of an opera called *Alceste*, which would have been produced at Covent Garden, Handel being engaged to write the music for it. All went well, and the work was actually in rehearsal, when Rich made some suggestions to Smollett about altering one of the scenes. Immediately the peppery poet was on his dignity. He declined to alter a line. Thereupon Rich, preferring to quarrel with his author rather than offend the public, rejected the piece, to Smollett's intense chagrin. In vain his friends begged of him to make some concession to Rich, who seems to have been exceedingly forbearing all through. The poet declined, and thus another chance of bettering his prospects was lost.

Handel, on hearing of the transaction, is reported to have remarked, 'That Scotchman is ein tam fool; I vould have mate his vurk immortal,' and immediately proceeded to alter the music so as to adapt it to Dryden's 'Ode for St. Cecilia's Day.' Verily *Alceste* would have been immortal if wedded to those noble harmonies. But it was not to be. The only result was the addition of another group of powerful social personages to his already long list of enemies, for of course Tobias could not refrain from lampooning Rich. 'O the pity of it!'

CHAPTER V

RODERICK RANDOM

We reach now the most important period of Smollett's life. That he had fully realised, long before, the splendid nature of the talents wherewith he was endowed, is more than probable, though he possibly was in doubt as to the precise outlet his genius would make for itself. He had tried tragedy, but had been roughly disillusionised as to his El Dorado being found on the stage. He had neither the power of compression nor the faculty of seizing upon one central idea and making all the others subservient and subordinate thereto, so necessary a qualification in the dramatist. His satire also was a little too ferocious and vitriolic to entirely please the taste of the English–reading public, that was gradually looking askance at the knockdown, sledge–hammer blows of Butler and Swift, and veering round to the more delicate but none the less effective style of Goldsmith, Gay, and Johnson. His poetry, moreover, was not sufficiently generous, either in quantity or quality, to secure for him even a low place in the Temple of Poesie. His genius, therefore, must find some other outlet. What was it to be?

In 1740, Samuel Richardson, the father of the English novel, had produced *Pamela*, a work which at once achieved a lasting success. Not that novel–writing was unknown previous to that date, as many writers suppose. The Italian *novelli* and the Spanish tales were known in Britain, and had inspired many imitators. While carefully dissociating the pastoral romances like Sidney's *Arcadia* or those 'romances' proper, or fiction dealing with feudal customs and illustrative of the 'virtues' of chivalry, from 'novels,' which, in the early signification of the word at least, implied stories descriptive of domestic or everyday life in the period of the writer's own immediate epoch, many of the stories written by Robert Greene, the dramatist, Thomas Nashe, and Nicolas Breton are novels of English life pure and simple, albeit foreign names may be used. So in Shakespeare all his plays are distinctively English in atmosphere and sympathies, to say nothing of sentiments, although Coriolanus, Julius Cæsar, Antony and Cleopatra, and the like, are selected as the nominal heroes and heroines of the piece. The English novel had long been in existence. The only difference was that the writers did not specialise any period as that wherein the incidents occurred. They preferred to leave themselves free, and to people with the creatures of their fancy that mysteriously delightful era vaguely shadowed forth by 'long ago' or 'once upon a time.'

The surpassing virtue of Richardson and his successor Fielding was that they boldly seized upon the time wherein they lived as that which was to form the background of their stories. Their 'to–day' was to be painted as faithfully and as fondly as those earlier writers had depicted imaginary epochs. We can scarcely form any idea now of the overwhelming enthusiasm that greeted Richardson's *Pamela*. For the first time readers saw their own age delineated with a fidelity and withal a fearlessness that had the effect of a supreme moral lesson. Of course, to our ideas of to–day, many of the descriptions in the novels of last century are simply revolting, and would be condemned amongst us as an outrage on good taste. 'The morals of the young person' are our nineteenth–century bogey, which ever and anon rises up to scare any luckless novelist who dares to paint life as it really is. Thackeray used to lament that he dared not paint Becky Sharp as she really was, because all the mammas in the British Islands would taboo his work. But midway the eighteenth century they were not so queasy–stomached. They called a spade a spade. If a man went to the devil with wine and women, they took a delight in chronicling the whole process—as a warning to others, be it noted, not like the leprous–minded, neurotic school in our own days, look you, because they wanted to rake in guineas by chronicling a brother's or a sister's shame.

Pamela, however, effected a higher purpose than merely affording pleasure to eager readers. Its exotic morality and exaggerated sentimentality stirred up into vigorous life the spirit of ridicule latent in the big, manly, kindly, but coarse–fibred nature of Henry Fielding. As a caricature of *Pamela* he produced his novel, *Joseph Andrews*, the hero of which was the brother of *Pamela*, and was made to exhibit the same exaggerated virtues as had characterised the latter. Fielding's "skit" became the first great character–novel in the English language, and announced to the world the fact that the greatest master of contemporary literary portraiture that prose literature has yet seen, had appeared.

The publication of *Clarissa Harlowe*, by Richardson, towards the end of 1747, and the announcement made of the appearance of Fielding's *Tom Jones*, in parts, seem to have raised the question in Smollett's mind whether he also might not be able to create a gallery of fiction every whit as notable as 'Pamela,' or 'Mr. B——,' or 'Parson Adams,' or 'Lovelace,' or 'Sophia Western.' The flattering results of success in the improvement of the material prospects of both Richardson and Fielding could not but exercise a certain amount of influence on him. In the month of June 1747, as he tells us, he began the composition of a novel of his own time, very diffidently, and with the resolve firmly kept in view, that if the work did not come up to his own expectations, he would remorselessly burn it.

He was of too original a caste of genius to sink into the subordinate position of a mere imitator of either Richardson or Fielding. He noted carefully that the former had monopolised the novel of sentiment, as the latter had taken as his own the novel of character. But he also saw that the novel of incident was still unappropriated in English fiction. This department he determined to make his own. Taking the *Gil Blas* of Le Sage as his model, he endeavoured as far as possible to make his tale interesting by the number and variety of the events introduced, feeling assured that the portraiture of character would not be of an inferior type, if only he could draw on his past experiences for material. While by no means a slavish follower of Le Sage, the influence of the great French writer is very perceptible in *Roderick Random*. There is the same breathless succession of incidents, the same hairbreadth escapes, the same ready ingenuity on the part of the hero in extricating himself from awkward predicaments. In a word, Roderick is but a blood relation of *Gil Blas*, though his British parentage and rearing have modified some of the eccentricities and peccadilloes that would have scared even the purblind mammas and custodians of national virtue last century.

Roderick Random was published towards the end of January 1748, having occupied five months in its composition. Its success was instant and extraordinary. The British public recognised that a third had been added to the great masters of fiction—a third whose genius, though inferior in solidity and sublimity to that of either Richardson or Fielding, surpassed both in prodigality and wealth of invention. The first edition of the work did not bear the author's name, but was published in two small duodecimo volumes by Osborn of Gray's Inn Lane (the same individual knocked down by Dr. Johnson as a punishment for insolence), the price being six shillings. The interest excited by the book may be imagined when it was attributed by Lady Mary Wortley Montague to Fielding. In a letter to her daughter, the Countess of Bute, as recorded in her works, Lady Mary says: 'Fielding has really a fund of true humour. I guessed *Roderick Random* to be his, though without his name.' Later on she adds: 'I cannot think *Ferdinand Fathom* wrote by the same hand, it is every way so much below it.'

The notices of the novel in any contemporary journals are but meagre. In the *Gentleman's Magazine* and in the *Intelligencer*, short criticisms appear noting it as a work 'full of ingenious descriptions and lively occurrences.' Several of the other periodicals contented themselves with a mere intimation of its publication. Of puffing and pushing seemingly the work needed little. Its own merits carried it into all circles. Even Samuel Richardson, whose antipathy to Fielding may have inclined him to show favour to any possible rival of the man who had dared to caricature his pet creation, remarked of it in comparison with *Tom Jones*, published some months later, that *Roderick Random* was written by a good man to show the evils of vice, *Tom Jones* by a profligate to render vice more alluring. The infallible judgment of posterity will not confirm the criticism of the narrow-minded old bookseller, who abhorred anything that did not directly or indirectly reflect praise on himself. Edition after edition of this the latest success in literature was called for. Smollett's name was placed on the title-page after the issue of the second edition, and the public then realised that the popular novel was the work of none of the elder writers, as was supposed, but of a young, impecunious surgeon, not yet thirty, who had exhibited a very pretty talent for satire, as the Dukes of Newcastle and Grafton, the Earls of Bath, Granville, and Cholmondeley, Sir William Yonge, Mr. Pitt, and Rich the theatrical manager, could testify to their cost.

Thereupon the town sought to take the young surgeon up and patronise him, only to discover that he was far from being a patronisable party—nay, was somewhat akin to the frozen snake which the countryman, pitying, took up and hid in his bosom to warm it, only to be stung when the reptile recovered vitality. Smollett all his life was too apt to mistake genuine kindness for patronage, and to flash out hasty darts of sarcasm in response to heartfelt wishes to win his friendship. Many of the leading personages of London now sought to benefit him and to show him that they desired to count him among their friends. But Tobias, as already said, was like the fretful porcupine. He had been so long a stranger to disinterested kindness, so long treated as little better than a superfluous atom on the world's surface, that affability towards him was construed into condescension—a thought which made each particular hair of his sensitive nature to stand on end. Curious though the fact, nevertheless it is true that Smollett's friendship was in most cases extended to those who differed from him rather than to those who agreed with him, though at the same time he might be bespattering the former with all the terms of reprobation in his somewhat extensive vocabulary of vituperation.

Although *Roderick Random*, coming, as it did, sandwiched in, so to speak, between *Clarissa Harlowe* and *Tom Jones*, had to pass through a trying fire of literary comparison, it emerged from the ordeal more popular than ever. Readers realised that in him was a writer who was a story–teller pure and simple, whose moral lessons were conveyed rather by implication than by positive precept, and to whom the progress of his story was the prime consideration. The wearisome moralisings of Richardson and the tedious untwistings of motive so characteristic of Fielding were unknown in *Roderick Random*. The story for the story's sake was evidently the writer's aim throughout, and nobly he fulfilled it. By many of our latter–day novelists the imaginative swiftness of Smollett might with advantage be studied.

All criticism will be reserved for our closing chapters, but at this point it may not be out of place to state that, although Smollett's characters are many of them drawn *from life*, it does not follow they are portrayed *to the life*. By this distinction I would seek to relieve him of the imputation, shameful in many cases beyond a doubt, of having deliberately drawn line for line the portraits of his relatives, of individuals met with on board the *Cumberland*, and other fellow–travellers with whom he had fallen in during his journey along the highway of existence. That suggestions were given to him by the actions of such men as the commander of the *Cumberland*, the staff of surgeons on board, and other personages with whom he came in contact, is perfectly probable. But that he noted through the microscope of his keen faculty of observation, every trait, every moral feature, and registered them on the debit or credit side of each character, I cannot admit, nor would such a course be consistent with the originality of his genius. The setting of incident may in some cases be drawn from his own experience, but that we can in any sense rely on each portrait in his works being a truthful representation of the prototype, that I deny. The assumption is negatived by his own confession with regard to his grandfather, and also by his action with reference to Gordon, his former employer. If the latter were drawn to the life under the character of either Potion or Crab in *Roderick Random*, as many biographers contend, Smollett completely ate his own words in *Humphrey Clinker* when he remarked that Gordon 'was a patriot of a truly noble spirit,' etc. There is nothing more misleading and at the same time more unfair to an author than to subject him to this sort of literary dissection. No author is without suggestions from without in limning his gallery of characters, but that he draws them wholly from without is as impossible as that a doctor's diagnosis is based solely on what he observes, or on what is visible to the eye, and not also on what is the result of arguing from the known to the unknown. Captains Oakum and Whiffle, Squire Gawky, and others, are intentionally exaggerated for the purposes of literary effect. If they were drawn from nature, then they would have to be severely condemned as exaggerations.

Sir Walter Scott speaks very decidedly on this point in *The Lives of the Novelists and Dramatists*: 'It was generally believed that Smollett painted some of his own early adventures under the veil of fiction; but the public carried the spirit of applying the characters of a work of fiction to living personages much farther than the author intended.' Dr. Moore, also, while acknowledging that Smollett was not sufficiently careful to prevent such applications of his characters, yet denies that they were portraits of living personages.

Smollett now could contemplate the future with hopefulness. *Roderick Random* had achieved a success so extraordinary, that even at that early period in his literary career, the booksellers, or, as they would now be termed, 'publishers,' were bespeaking his wares ahead. Taken all in all, Smollett accepted his good fortune with conspicuous moderation. Success did not turn his head. He was not like his characters, Roderick Random or Peregrine Pickle, extravagantly uplifted by prosperity, plunged into despair by adversity. More akin to worthy old Matthew Bramble was he, who, while he took the world at no very high valuation, and was not averse to accepting its smile, yet did not break his heart over its frown.

The only foolish action to which he gave way at this period of popularity was the publication by subscription of *The Regicide*. The fame accruing to him from the success of his novel was, he reasoned, a favourable means whereby to enable him to launch his play upon the waters of public opinion. His reputation certainly ensured the sale of his play, but the sale of his play materially affected his reputation. That *The Regicide* was not a work of merit Smollett never could be brought to see, until he had criticised for some years the works of others in the *Critical Review*. Besides, he had sufficient of the old Adam in him that he wished 'to have his knife' into the offending theatrical managers, and the 'great little men,' as he called them, who had professed to take his play under their patronage. Therefore, when *The Regicide* was published in 1749, our author prefixed thereto a preface full of gall and vinegar—a piece of spleen, of which, in his later days, he was sincerely ashamed. That preface is not pleasant reading to those who love the genius of Smollett. A vindictive schoolboy in the first flush of resentment against his teacher for giving him a sound but deserved birching could not have perpetrated anything much worse.

In 1750, Smollett and his wife paid a visit to Paris, in order that the popular novelist might collect materials for his new work of fiction. The charms of the gay city, the kindness and consideration shown him by the Parisians, the adulation showered on him by the literary men of the French capital, all coloured Smollett's estimate of the place and people. 'To live in Paris,' he says in one of his letters of the period, 'is to live in heaven.' That he saw reason slightly to alter his opinion afterwards, was only to be expected. But the delights of this first visit to Paris remained indelibly impressed on his memory.

He met many persons in France whose characters and circumstances afterwards suggested to him some of the most notable personages in his gallery of fiction. For example, Moore, in his memoirs of Smollett, states that the portrait of the Doctor in *Peregrine Pickle* was drawn in some respects from Dr. Akenside, the well–known poet, author of *The Pleasures of Imagination*, a man of true learning, culture, and high talents, but whose offence, in Smollett's eyes, was that he had cast some sneering reflections upon Scotland in Smollett's presence, although, on the other hand, Akenside had studied in Edinburgh, and acknowledged the excellence of its medical school. Pallet the painter, also, was suggested to him, adds Moore, by the coxcombry of an English artist, who used to declaim on the subject of *Virtu*, and often used the following expressions, familiar enough to readers of the novel in question—'Paris is very rich in the arts; London is a Goth, and Westminster a Vandal, compared to Paris.'

But the most effective episode drawn by Smollett from his French experiences was, as Anderson says, the story of the Scottish Jacobite exiles, banished from their country for their share in the Rebellion of 1745. Readers of *Peregrine Pickle* will remember that at Boulogne the hero meets a body of these unfortunates, who daily made a pilgrimage to the seaside to view the white cliffs of Britain, which they were never more to approach. That incident was drawn from life. Mr. Hunter of Burnside was the individual amongst them who is mentioned as having wept bitterly over his misfortune of having involved a beloved wife and three children in misery and distress, and in the impatience of his grief, having cursed his fate with frantic imprecations. Dr. Moore heard Mr. Hunter express himself in this manner to Smollett, and at the same time relate the affecting visit which he and his companions daily made to the seaside when residing at Boulogne. From his visit, then, Smollett drew a wealth of incidents and characteristics, which he was able with surpassing skill to touch up, recolour, magnify, and exaggerate as he saw fit in the interests of his story.

At this period, John Home, author of *Douglas*, was paying a visit to London in order to try to induce Garrick to accept his tragedy of *Agis*. He met Smollett, introduced to him by their mutual friend 'Jupiter' Carlyle, and had much pleasant intercourse with him. From the Life[5] of Home by Henry Mackenzie, I extract the following details, as they throw a curious side–light on Smollett's character. In his letter, dated 6th November 1749, to Carlyle, he remarks: 'I have seen nobody yet but Smollett, whom I like very well.' Farther on he adds: 'I am a good deal disappointed at the mien of the English, which I think but poor. I observed it to Smollett, after having walked at High–Mall, who agreed with me.' Then, a little later, Home writes to 'Jupiter,' evidently grateful for some kindnesses shown him by Tobias, in the following terms:—'Your friend Smollett, who has a thousand good, nay, the best qualities, and whom I love much more than he thinks I do, has got on Sunday last three hundred pounds for his *Mask*.' What this *Mask* was it is hard to say, but in all probability it referred to some work which Smollett was executing for Garrick. To the *Alceste* the allusion could not refer, nor to the *Reprisals*. The allusion, therefore, must be directed to some cobbling dramatic work, of which Smollett did a great deal for Drury Lane, Covent Garden, and Goodman's Fields.

A testimony so independent as this from Home possesses the highest value. To the virtues and excellences of a much misunderstood man it offers a tardy but valuable vindication.

Of Smollett, David Hume, who met him somewhat later in life, said: 'He is like the cocoa–nut, the outside is the worst part of him.'

CHAPTER VI

Both during his stay in Paris, and on his return, Smollett had been working steadily at his new novel, which he had called *The Adventures of Peregrine Pickle*. The title of all his books affords a clue to their character. Incident—vigorous, well described incident, lively, incessant, exhaustless—such was the 'mode' of fiction our author had determined to make his own. Hence the titles of his works—*The Adventures of Roderick Random, The Adventures of Peregrine Pickle, The Adventures of Ferdinand Count Fathom, The Adventures of Sir Launcelot Greaves, The Expedition of Humphrey Clinker*—are genuinely descriptive of his style of writing. He had no patience for the slow analysis of character, or the exhibition of wire–drawn sentiments. His novels were always on the boil. There was no cooling down of the interest permitted, even for a moment. No sooner was the hero done with one incident than another was hard on its trail to overtake him. Ennui and dullness have a bad time of it while one of Smollett's novels is in course of perusal.

In 1750, acting upon the urgent solicitations of his wife, he made a last attempt to establish himself as a physician. Mrs. Smollett did not exactly appreciate a husband who had no profession. Poor Nancy does not seem to have been a very suitable yokefellow for our busy *litterateur*. She had no reverence for literature as such, or for its professors. She had all a woman's desire for social distinction. But in order to take any position in that society after which this poor little Eve of the eighteenth century panted as eagerly as those of the nineteenth, an indispensable desideratum was that her husband should belong to one of the recognised professions, even although it might be only 'something in the City'! To hope to settle in London was out of the question. That had been already tried, and had failed. Perhaps the good folks of the city of King Bladud might be more amenable to the recommendations of Dr. Smollett's skill. Therefore Smollett resolved to settle at Bath, and see whether he could gain a living as a doctor at the great eighteenth century Spa.

Before this project could be put into practice, however, medical etiquette demanded he should take a physician's degree. Hitherto he only had secured a surgeon's certificate, and that was of little service at Bath. Accordingly, he proceeded to take his degree of M.D., and thereafter had a right to sign himself 'Dr. Smollett.' Considerable doubt existed formerly regarding the University whence our author obtained his diploma. Even so late as in Dr. Anderson's time (1805–1820, the dates of the editions of his book), the question had not been decided. The statement in his Life of Smollett that his diploma was probably obtained from some foreign University, and that 'the researches which have hitherto been made in the lists of graduates in the Scottish Universities, have not discovered his name,' led investigators to every other quarter but the right one. All the registers of the foreign medical schools were ransacked in vain. To Sir Walter Scott must be ascribed the honour of settling the matter once for all, by proving that Smollett was a medical graduate of Aberdeen. Let Sir Walter speak for himself. He says: 'The late ingenious artist, Mr. H. W. Williams of Edinburgh, tells us in his *Travels*, that a friend of his had seen in 1816, at Leghorn, the diploma of Smollett's doctorate, and that it was an Aberdeen one. The present editor thought it worth while to inquire into this, and Professor Cruikshank has politely forwarded a certificated copy of the diploma, which was granted by the Marischal College of Aberdeen in 1750.' Accordingly, therefore, for a year or two at least, we must picture the author of *Roderick Random* feeling the pulses and examining the tongues of patients who, in many cases, were mere valetudinarians, or, on the other hand, feigned themselves ill that they might have an excuse for visiting the gay city of Bath. With that irritating class of patients Smollett would have no patience. He would brusquely expose their petty deceit; and in one case, at least, informed a lady that 'if she had time to play at being ill, he had not time to play at curing her.' Such a physician was like a wild buffalo let loose over the conventional *parterres* of the sentimental femininity of both sexes. He simply gored with his rude satire the pleasant fictions of lusty but lazy invalids, or scattered to the winds the fond delusions of hypochondriacs, in whom too much old port and high living had induced the demons of dyspepsia. Little wonder is it, then, that Smollett as a physician was as supreme a failure as Oliver Goldsmith. Within two years we find him back in London, cursing his folly in ever having been induced to try an experiment that was doomed to failure from the very outset. Alas, poor little Mrs. Smollett! her dreams of social importance were rudely dispelled. From a brief experience of playing 'the doctor's dame' among the good folks of Bath, she had ignominiously to return to London and sink into the obscurity of a lady who cannot even aspire to the credit of having a husband who is 'something in the City.' In 'Narcissa's' eyes—for there is little doubt that the character of Narcissa in *Roderick Random* was at least suggested by his wife—her husband's literary work was worse than degrading. In common with many others of her time, she deemed 'a man of letters' to be synonymous with a gentleman who spent one–half his time in the Fleet or the Marshalsea for debt, and the other half in dodging bailiffs from post to pillar for the privilege of enjoying God's sunshine without the walls of a jail.

One piece of work Smollett accomplished before he left Bath. He published a short treatise on the mineral waters of the place under the title, *An Essay on the External Use of Water, in a letter to Dr.——, with Particular Remarks on the Present Method of Using the Mineral Waters at Bath in Somersetshire, and a Plan for rendering them more Safe, Agreeable, and Efficacious* (4to, 1752). The book is full of sound maxims for the preservation of health. But here and there he cannot resist girding at those who visited the place for no other purpose than to participate in its gaieties, and whose ailments were as fictitious as in many cases was their social standing. This was, of course, a hit at the crowds of sharpers and adventurers of all sorts, male and female, that frequented Bath during its palmy days last century.

While at Bath, however, that is, in March 1751, *Peregrine Pickle*, his second great novel, was published in two volumes duodecimo, the imprint being 'London: Printed for the Author, and Sold by D. Wilson, at Plato's Head, near Round Court in the Strand, 1751.' This implies that Smollett had found the method more to his advantage to act as his own publisher, than to submit to the extortion of the greedy Shylocks of the press in those days. The race of great publishers, taking a genuine interest in their authors and their work, had yet to arise—that race of which Scott's friend Constable was one of the earliest examples and the best.

The success of the new novel was unparalleled. As Herbert says in his excellent prefatory Life to the Works of Smollett: 'It was received with such extraordinary avidity that a large impression was quickly sold in England, another was bought up in Ireland, a translation was executed into the French language, and it soon made its appearance in a second edition with an apologetic *Advertisement* and *Two Letters* relating to the *Memoirs of a Lady of Quality*, sent to the editor by "a Person of Honour." This first edition is in our day scarce enough, and sufficiently coarse to fetch an enhanced price.' Edition followed edition of the popular work. If any doubt had previously existed whether Smollett was worthy to take his place beside Richardson and Fielding, none could be urged now. In all contemporary records we find the three bracketed together, as the great fictional trio whose works were at once the delight and the despair of imitators.

But although his career was so successful, we must not run away with the idea that Smollett had no enemies—that, in a word, admiration had swallowed up animosity. Alas, no! Human nature is human nature through all. Despite all the *furore* of enthusiasm awakened by the appearance of his great novel, there were not lacking detractors and vilifiers, who, too despicable to attack him openly, snapped at him from under the shield of anonymity. That they were able to do him harm, or at least to cause him keen chagrin and vexation, is made manifest by the tone of sorrow and wounded pride wherewith he speaks in the preface to the second edition of *Peregrine Pickle*. In such circumstances it is always best to let the aggrieved party speak for himself without offering any opinion. He says: 'At length *Peregrine Pickle* makes his appearance in a new edition, in spite of all the art and industry that were used to stifle him in the birth by certain booksellers and others, who were at uncommon pains to misrepresent the work and calumniate the author. The performance was decried as an immoral piece, and a scurrilous libel; the author was charged with having defamed the characters of particular persons to whom he lay under considerable obligations; and some formidable critics declared the book was void of humour, character, and sentiment. These charges, had they been supported by proof, would have certainly damned the writer and all his works; and, even unsupported as they were, had an unfavourable effect with the public. But luckily for him his real character was not unknown; and some readers were determined to judge for themselves, rather than trust implicitly to the allegations of his enemies. He has endeavoured to render the book less unworthy of their acceptance. Divers uninteresting incidents are wholly suppressed. Some humorous scenes he has endeavoured to heighten; and he flatters himself he has expunged every adventure, phrase, and insinuation that could be construed by the most delicate reader into a trespass upon the rules of decorum. He owns with contrition that in one or two instances he gave way too much to the suggestions of personal resentment, and represented characters as they appeared to him at that time through the exaggerating medium of prejudice. However he may have erred in point of judgment or discretion, he defies the whole world to prove that he was ever guilty of one act of malice, ingratitude, or dishonour. This declaration he may be permitted to make, without incurring the imputation of vanity or presumption, considering the numerous shafts of envy, rancour, and revenge that have lately, both in public and private, been levelled at his reputation.'

Along with the *Adventures* of Peregrine were bound up *Memoirs of a Lady of Quality*—a distinct story, sandwiched, as it were, between the two halves of the hero's life. Clumsy indeed is the fictional skill that permitted such an arrangement. The introduction of the *Memoirs*, apart altogether from their moral quality, was a constructive error, inasmuch as the thread of interest of the novel is thereby broken. Though Smollett received a handsome sum (£150 one account mentions, £300 another) for granting the favour of their insertion in the novel, he lived to regret most deeply the indiscretion. So notorious was the reputation of the lady, that her infamous character in some people's estimation condemned the book. The 'Lady of Quality,' as is well known, was the unhappy Lady Vane. Her maiden name was Frances Hawes. She was married when little more than a child to Lord William Hamilton, who died shortly afterwards; then to Viscount Vane, who used her with such cruelty that she was driven to accept the protection of the Hon. Sewallis Shirley, son of Robert, first Earl of Ferrers; then that of Lord Berkeley, Lord Robert Bertie, and others. Of course we have only her ladyship's side of the story. From other sources, however, information is forthcoming that she had been at least as much sinned against as sinning. But although the world may acknowledge thus much, it will never forgive a woman the breach of her marriage vows, and Lady Vane, although undoubtedly the most beautiful woman of her decade, has passed into a byword of reproach. Dr. Johnson in the *Vanity of Human Wishes* remarks:

'Yet Vane could tell what ills from beauty spring,
And Sedley cursed the form that pleased a king.'

But undoubtedly the quality which most of all recommended *Peregrine Pickle* to the British public was the marvellously true, albeit richly humorous, portraits of our seamen in the persons of Commodore Hawser Trunnion, Lieutenant Hatchway, and Boatswain Tom Pipes. It is questionable, however, if any of those exhibited so much insight into the human heart as that of Lieutenant Bowling in *Roderick Random*, a noble–spirited man if ever one was created. Smollett has since had many imitators, such as Captain Marryat, Mr. Clark Russell, and others, but none of them have excelled the inimitable wit and humour which invest the sayings and doings of these personages. They have become part and parcel of ourselves. We know them and love them, and they live with us, so to speak, in our daily life.

He now took up house in Chelsea, and set himself doggedly and perseveringly to obtain his subsistence as a professional man of letters. From the Government of the day he could look for no favours. The unmerciful manner in which he had lashed the Ministry, says Chambers, precluded all Court patronage, even had it been the fashion of the Court of George II. to extend it. He depended solely on the booksellers for whom he wrought in the various departments of compilations, translations, criticisms, and miscellaneous essays.

The next fruit of his genius was one which has never been popular, simply because it describes an utterly impossible and repulsive character. In 1753 appeared *The Adventures of Ferdinand Count Fathom*. A more depressing and unhealthy work, despite the immense genius displayed in it, could scarcely be conceived. Sir Walter Scott's analysis of the novel is so admirable that we cannot do better than cite it here in place of any lengthened remarks of our own. 'It seems to have been written for the purpose of showing how far humour and genius can go in painting a complete picture of human depravity.... To a reader of good disposition and well–regulated mind, the picture of moral depravity presented in the character of Count Fathom is a disgusting pollution of the imagination. To those, on the other hand, who hesitate on the brink of meditated iniquity, it is not safe to detail the arts by which the ingenuity of villainy has triumphed in former instances; and it is well known that the publication of the real account of uncommon crimes, although attended by the public and infamous punishment of the perpetrators, has often had the effect of stimulating others to similar actions.'

But if the moral features of Count Fathom are thus repulsive, there can be no question of the supreme art wherewith the developments of such a character are both conceived and executed. The heartless villainy wherewith Fathom executes his devilish schemes are related with a subdued force that is unlike anything else in fiction; while the scene of the ruin of the unfortunate Monimia is one of the most terribly dramatic passages in the English language, comparable only to the terrible remorse scene in *Macbeth*, or to the great last act in Webster's *Duchess of Malfi*. The horror is if anything overstrained. One recoils from it. It leaves an impression on the mind as though human nature were utterly debased and vicious, without a single redeeming trait. The novel once more achieved a great success. Though its weak points were indicated by the critics of the day, their objections had no influence on the popularity of the book.

The dedication of the novel can refer to no other individual than himself, because to no other whose friendship he valued would he dare use the language he employs. The work is inscribed to Dr. * * * and his own failings of character are therein inscribed with rare fidelity. 'Know, then, I can despise your pride while I honour your integrity, and applaud your taste while I am shocked at your ostentation. I have known you trifling, superficial, and obstinate in dispute; meanly jealous and awkwardly reserved; rash and haughty in your resentments; and coarse and lowly in your connections. I have blushed at the weakness of your conversation, and trembled at the errors of your conduct. Yet, as I own you possess certain good qualities which overbalance these defects and distinguish you on this occasion as a person for whom I have the most perfect attachment and esteem, you have no cause to complain of the indelicacy with which your faults are reprehended; and as they are chiefly the excesses of a sanguine disposition and looseness of thought, impatient of caution and control, you may, thus stimulated, watch over your own intemperance and infirmity with redoubled vigilance and consideration; and for the future profit by the severity of my reproof.' From this, one would gather that Smollett was quite cognisant of his own weakness of temper—a weakness from which many of us suffer, but few of us are quite so honest as to own!

The publication of *Count Fathom* was the indirect means of involving Smollett in an unpleasant affair, from which he was not extricated without some trouble. Warmth of temper again! A countryman, Peter Gordon, had got into difficulties and was brought to the verge of ruin, when Smollett came to his rescue, and, with more humanity than worldly wisdom, became security for him. Presently Gordon took sanctuary within the King's Bench Prison, and sent defiant and insolent messages to Smollett when the latter appealed to his sense of honour to repay him his losses. This conduct so provoked the choleric Smollett, that on meeting the rascal he soundly caned him. Thereupon the latter raised an action against him in the Court of the King's Bench, exaggerating the assault into attempted murder. Gordon's counsel was a lawyer afterwards infamous in many senses, the Hon. Alexander Hume–Campbell, twin brother of Pope's Earl of Marchmont. He opened the case for his client with a speech full of disgraceful and unwarranted abuse of Smollett. The jury, however, acquitted the latter from any blame in the matter beyond common assault, probably considering in their hearts that Gordon only received what he richly deserved. But Smollett felt keenly the innuendoes cast upon his character by Campbell. He therefore sent to his friend Daniel Mackercher—already familiar to us as the Mr. M—— of *Peregrine Pickle*—a long letter addressed to Campbell, expostulating with him upon his conduct, demanding an apology, and in the event of it not being forthcoming, threatening a challenge. The whole action was foolish. Probably Mackercher acted as a wise friend in the matter, by advising him not to send the epistle. At any rate, we hear no more of the matter, and Smollett had relieved his feelings by abusing his enemy—behind his back. Long years afterwards, the letter appeared in the *European Magazine*. But both the principals were dead!

CHAPTER VII

VISIT TO SCOTLAND—*THE CRITICAL REVIEW*—*THE REPRISAL*. 1755–1759.

Smollett was from this time forward plunged into a sea of pecuniary troubles, wherein, with little mitigation, he remained as long as life lasted. The year 1754, wherein he had to meet the costs of the action for assault brought against him by Gordon, seems to have been the one wherein his distresses culminated. For some time he was in danger of arrest. He skulked about London like 'a thief at large,' ever afraid of feeling a hand on his shoulder, and of beholding a bailiff ready to conduct him to the 'sponging–house.' For some years his monetary difficulties, like a snowball, had been always increasing. In his Life of Smollett, Dr. Robert Chambers has drawn a painful picture of the great genius fretting like some noble steed condemned to pack–horse duty, at the unworthy tasks he was obliged to undertake. Yet five out of every six of his embarrassments were the result of his own folly and extravagance. A man has to cut his coat according to his cloth. Smollett would never consent to exercise present economy to avoid future embarrassment. In a letter dated 1752 he complains of lack of money through failure of his West India revenue. The income from his wife's property was now greatly decreased, while what remained was frittered away on vexatious lawsuits. 'Curse the law!' he cried impatiently on one occasion, 'it has damned more honest men to lifelong drudgery than anything else.' In another letter, in May 1753, addressed to his friend Dr. Macaulay, he acknowledges having received a previous loan of £15, but begs for the favour of another £50 to save him from serious difficulty. He promises payment from the proceeds of some work he then had in hand, probably *Don Quixote*. By a bankruptcy he had lost £180, and was obliged to immediately discount a note of hand of Provost Drummond's, at a sacrifice of sixty per cent., in place of waiting for the due–date. In December 1754 he again laments the failure of remittances from Jamaica and of actual extremities. So far down was he, that he was compelled to write to his brother–in–law, Mr. Telfer, begging the favour of a loan, which after some delay he received. All these accumulated distresses weighed upon his spirits. 'My life is sheer slavery,' he wrote to one of his friends; 'my pen is at work from nine o' the clock the one morning until one or two the next. I might as well be in Grub Street.' Still he toiled on, though he realised that the work he was doing was far from being worthy of him. As Anderson says: 'The booksellers were his principal resource for employment and subsistence; for them he held the pen of a ready writer in the walk of general literature, and towards him they were as liberal as the patronage of the public enabled them to be. They were almost his only patrons; and, indeed, a more generous set of men can hardly be pointed out in the trading world. By their liberality, wit and learning have perhaps received more ample and more substantial encouragement than from all their princely and noble patrons.'

Darker and ever darker grows the picture. Whether or not Mrs. Smollett was a poor housewife, or whether Smollett's own extravagances were wholly to blame, certain it is that from the period we have now reached until his not unwelcome release from life came in 1771, there was no ease for the toiling hand, no rest for the weary brow of the great novelist. His daily 'darg' had to be accomplished whether in sickness or in health; his daily tale of bricks to be handed in, if the rod of poverty's stern task–mistress was to be averted from his shoulders, or the wolf of want driven from the door. But, alas, at what an expenditure of brain tissue was it achieved! He knew he was unable to take time to produce his best work, and the saddening consciousness weighed ever more heavily upon him. In March 1755, accordingly, there appeared his translation of the *History of the Renowned Don Quixote; from the Spanish of Miguel de Cervantes Saavedra, with some Account of the Author's life, illustrated with 28 new copperplates, designed by Hayman and engraved by the best Artists*. The volumes, which were in quarto, were two in number, and were issued by Rivington, being dedicated by permission to Don Ricardo Wall, Principal Secretary of State to His Most Catholic Majesty, who, while he was resident in London as Spanish Ambassador, had exhibited much interest in the work. Though accomplished Spanish scholars, according to Moore, have accused Smollett of not having had a sufficient knowledge of the language when he undertook the task, for to perform it perfectly it would be requisite that the translator had lived some years in Spain, that he had obtained not only a knowledge of the Court and of polite society, but an acquaintance also with the vulgar idioms, the proverbs in use among the populace, and the various customs of the country to which allusions are made; still the fact remains that Smollett's translation has never been superseded, and that it at once threw into the shade the previous renderings of Motteux and Jervis. Lord Woodhouselee, in his *Essay on the Principles of Translation*, has endeavoured, with a strange perversity of taste, to depreciate Smollett's version in favour of that of Motteux. But the verdict of time has proved how egregiously he was in the wrong. Smollett's short 'Advertisement' to the work manifests the principles according to which he prosecuted his translation. He states that his 'aim in this undertaking was to maintain that ludicrous solemnity and self–importance by which the inimitable Cervantes has distinguished the character of Don Quixote, without raising him to the insipid rank of a dry philosopher or debasing him to the melancholy circumstances and unentertaining caprice of an ordinary madman; to preserve the native humour of Sancho Panza from degenerating into mere proverbial phlegm or affected buffoonery; that the author has endeavoured to retain the spirit and ideas without servilely adhering to the literal expressions of the original, from which, however, he has not so far deviated as to destroy that formality of idiom so peculiar to the Spaniards, and so essential to the character of the work.' It is not often that genius is brought to the service of translation. When it is, however, as in the case of Lord Berners' *Froissart* and Smollett's *Don Quixote*, the result is memorable. Smollett, alas! reaped little immediate benefit from its publication. The work had been contracted and paid for five years before!

No sooner did he get this portion of his stipulated labour off his hands, than he determined to visit his relatives in Scotland. His heart yearned to see his mother. Fifteen years had passed since the raw lad, with his tragedy in his pocket, had set out for London, as he fondly hoped, conquering and to conquer. He now returned to his native country the pale, weary, toil–worn man, older–looking than his years by at least a decade. Dr. Moore relates the pathetic scene of the recognition of her celebrated son by the aged mother, then living with her daughter, Mrs. Telfer, at Scotston. Let us quote Dr. Moore's words: 'With the connivance of Mrs. Telfer, on his arrival, he was introduced to his mother as a gentleman from the West Indies who had been intimately acquainted with her son. The better to support his assumed character, he endeavoured to preserve a very serious countenance, approaching a frown; but while the old lady's eyes were riveted with a kind of wild and eager stare on his countenance, he could not refrain from smiling. She immediately sprang from her chair, and, throwing her arms around his neck, exclaimed, "Ah, my son, my son, I have found you at last." She afterwards told him that if he had kept his austere look, and continued to *gloom*, as she called it, he might have escaped detection some time longer; "but your old roguish smile," added she, "betrayed you at once."'

Smollett returned to his native country under very different circumstances from those under which he left it. Then, his family connections were anxious to get rid of him, rejoiced, in fact, to see him launched upon any profession that would remove him from their midst. He left, a poor, lonely, depressed, yet at the same time high–spirited lad, eating his heart out owing to the necessity for showing respect to those who lacked the one claim to it acknowledged by him—intellectual eminence. Now he returned, the most popular, perhaps, for the time being, of any of the three great masters of British fiction—a 'lion,' with whom to hold intercourse was an honour indeed. That Smollett was not wholly without feelings of this nature, his letters evince. 'I have returned a little better than when I set out,' he is reported to have said to John Home as they walked together down the Canongate of Edinburgh.

His reception in the Scots metropolis, from which Scotston is distant only some twenty–three miles, was gratifying in the extreme. Smollett had the advantage of seeing the town in all its antiquity before the migration of the better classes took place to George Square and to 'the New Town' across the Nor' Loch. In 1756 it was still the quaint, formal, interesting, self–assertive place it had been before the Union in 1707. Here is a description of it by Gilbert Elliot, one of the Lords of the Admiralty, and one of the few friends Smollett had who were connected with the Government. 'I love the town tolerably well; there is one fine street, and the houses are extremely high. The gentry are a very sensible set of people, and some of them in their youth seem to have known the world; but by being too long in a place their notions are contracted and their faces are become solemn. The Faculty of Advocates is a very learned and a very worthy body. As for the ladies, they are unexceptionable, innocent, beautiful, and of an easy conversation. The staple vices of the place are censoriousness and hypocrisy. There is here no allowance for levity, none for dissipation. I am not a bit surprised I do not find here that unconstrained noble way of thinking and talking which one every day meets with among young fellows of plentiful fortunes and good spirits, who are constantly moving in a more enlarged circle of company.'

With Dr. 'Jupiter' Carlyle of Inveresk he renewed that acquaintance begun some years before, when neither of them had attained the fame that came to them in the course of time. Carlyle introduced him to many of his influential friends, and, in consequence, Smollett's visit to Edinburgh proved an exceedingly happy one. 'It was also in one of these days that Smollett visited Scotland for the first time,' says Carlyle, 'after having left Glasgow immediately after his education was finished, and his engaging as a surgeon's mate on board a man–of–war, which gave him an opportunity of witnessing the siege of Carthagena, which he has so minutely described in his *Roderick Random*. He came out to Musselburgh and passed a day and a night with me, and went to church and heard me preach. I introduced him to Cardonnel the Commissioner (of Customs), with whom he supped, and they were much pleased with each other. Smollett has reversed this in his *Humphrey Clinker*, where he makes the Commissioner his old acquaintance. He went next to Glasgow and that neighbourhood to visit his friends, and returned again to Edinburgh in October, when I had frequent meetings with him, one in particular in a tavern, where there supped with him and Commissioner Cardonnel, Mr. Hepburn of Keith, John Home, and one or two more.... Cardonnel and I went with Smollett to Sir David Kinloch's and passed the day, when John Home and Logan and I conducted him to Dunbar, where we stayed together all night.'

Smollett's picture of the Edinburgh of his time in *Humphrey Clinker* is exceedingly graphic. 'In the evening we arrived,' writes Melford, 'at this metropolis, of which I can say but very little. It is very romantic from its situation on the declivity of a hill, having a fortified castle at the top and a royal palace at the bottom. The first thing that strikes the nose of a stranger shall be nameless; but what first strikes the eye is the unconscionable height of the houses, which generally rise to five, six, seven, and eight storeys, and in some cases, as I am assured, to twelve. This manner of building, attended by numberless inconveniences, must have been originally owing to want of room. Certain it is the town seems to be full of people.' In the next letter Matthew Bramble adds: 'Every storey is a complete house occupied by a separate family, and the stair being common to them all is generally left in a very filthy condition; a man must tread with great circumspection to get safe housed with unpolluted shoes. Nothing, however, can form a stronger contrast between the outside and inside of the door, for the good women of this metropolis are very nice in the ornaments and propriety of their apartments, as if they were resolved to transfer the imputation from the individual to the public. You are no stranger to their method of discharging all their impurities from their windows at a certain hour of the night, as the custom is in Spain, Portugal, and other parts of France and Italy; a practice to which I can by no means be reconciled, for, notwithstanding all the care that is taken by their scavengers to remove this nuisance every morning by break of day, enough still remains to offend the eyes as well as the other organs of those whom use has not hardened against all delicacy of sensation.' Nor can we omit what the inimitable Winnifred Jenkins—the prototype and model of all future *soubrettes* in fiction—says on the subject: 'And now, dere Mary, we have got to Haddingborough (Edinburgh) among the Scots, who are cevel enuff for our money, thof I don't speak their lingo. But they should not go for to impose on foreigners, for the bills on their houses say they have different *easements* to let; but behold there is nurra geaks in the whole kingdom, nor anything for pore sarvants, but a barril with a pair of tongs thrown across, and all the chairs in the family are emptied into this here barril once a day, and at ten o'clock at night the whole cargo is flung out of a back windore that looks into some street or lane, and the Made cries "Gardyloo" to the passengers, which signerfies, "Lord have mercy upon you," and this is done every night in every house in Haddingborough, so you may guess, Mary Jones, what a sweet savour comes from such a number of profuming pans. But they say it is wholesome; and truly I believe it is; for being in the vapours and thinking of Issabel (Jezabel) and Mr. Clinker, I was going into a fit of astericks when this fiff, saving your presence, took me by the nose so powerfully that I sneezed three times and found myself wonderfully refreshed; this, to be sure, is the raisin why there are no fits in Haddingborough.'

From Edinburgh, Smollett, as we have seen, proceeded to Dumbartonshire, and then to Glasgow. His cousin was still laird of Bonhill, and welcomed him with much warmth back to the scene of his early years. In Glasgow he renewed his acquaintance with Dr. Moore, who had succeeded him as apprentice with Mr. Gordon, and was now a physician of repute in the western metropolis. With the latter he remained two days, renewing old associations both at the College and elsewhere. Unfortunately, very little information can be gleaned regarding this visit of Smollett's to Glasgow. Moore dismisses it in two or three lines, and every succeeding biographer, Anderson, Walter Scott, Chambers, Herbert, and Hannay, although mayhap spinning out a few more sentences, really do not add a tittle to our facts.

On returning to Edinburgh in October, he was welcomed by all the *literati* of the capital, and was specially invited to a meeting of the famous *Select Society*,[6] first mooted by Allan Ramsay the painter, as Mr. John Rae tells us in his *Life of Adam Smith*; but the fifteen original members of which had increased well–nigh to a hundred, comprising all the best–known names in literature, philosophy, science, and the arts. There he met or saw Kames and Monboddo (not yet 'paper lords' or lords of Session), Robertson and Ferguson and Hume, Carlyle and John Home, Dr. Blair, Wilkie of the *Epigoniad*, Wallace the statistician, Islay Campbell and Thomas Miller of the Court of Session, the Earls of Sutherland, Hopetoun, Marchmont, Morton, Rosebery, Errol, Aboyne, Cassilis, Selkirk, Glasgow, and Lauderdale; Lords Elibank, Gray, Garlies, Auchinleck, and Hailes; John Adam the architect, Dr. Cullen, John Coutts the banker, and many others.[7] The Society met every Friday evening from six to nine, at first in a room in the Advocates' Library, but when that became too small for the numbers that began to attend its meetings, in a room hired from the Masonic Lodge above the Laigh Council House; and its debates, in which the younger advocates and ministers, men like Wedderburn and Robertson, took the chief part, became speedily famous over all Scotland, as intellectual displays to which neither the General Assembly of the Kirk nor the Imperial Parliament could show anything to rival.

On returning to London, Smollett at once threw himself into the feverish excitement and worry of a journalistic life. In other words, he assumed the editorship of the new *Critical Review*, representative of High Church and Tory principles. This periodical, with its older rival, the *Monthly Review* (started by Griffiths in 1749 as the Whig organ), may be considered the prototypes of that plentiful crop of monthly magazines wherewith we are furnished to–day. The *Critical Review* was the property of a man named Hamilton, a Scotsman, whose enlightenment and liberality, remarks Herbert, had been proved by his listening to Chatterton's request for a little money, by sending it to him and telling him he should have more if he wanted it. The *Critical Review* for its age was really a very creditable production, though there was little to choose between the rivals as to merit, for the *Monthly*, at the date of the founding of its antagonist, was edited by a young man of surpassing ability, who won for himself a name in English literature even more distinguished than Smollett's—Oliver Goldsmith. Thus the authors of the *Vicar of*

Wakefield and of *Peregrine Pickle*—compositions wide as the poles apart in character—were thrown into rivalry with each other. That it was a rivalry embittered by any of the rancour and acrimony distinguishing Smollett's future journalistic relations with John Wilkes, cannot be supposed, inasmuch as Goldsmith contributed several articles to the *Critical Review*, and as a return compliment Smollett four, at least, to the *Monthly*. The proprietors of the opposing periodicals may have had their squabbles and bespattered each other with foul names, but the editors seem to have been on the most amicable of terms and to have united in anathematising both parties.

Much of Smollett's time was frittered away on work for the *Review* which would have been more remuneratively employed in other fields. But the pot had to be kept boiling, and there was but little fuel in reserve wherewith to feed the fire. He was far from making an ideal editor,—indeed, to tell the plain truth, he made an exceedingly bad one. He never kept his staff of contributors in hand. They were permitted to air their own grievances and to revenge their own quarrels in the *Review*. His criticisms, also, are very one–sided. The remarks on John Home's *Douglas*, though true so far, are much too sweeping in their generalisations. The play has many merits, but the *Critical Review* would fain persuade one it had next to none. The same remarks are true of Wilkie's *Epigoniad*, by no means a work of great genius, but deserving better things said of it than the *Critical* meted out. With respect to the criticism on Dr. Grainger, the writer simply displayed the grossest and most culpable ignorance and impertinence towards the productions of a learned and refined Englishman. In a word, the injustice, the intemperance of language, and the inexcusable blunders which characterised Smollett's occupancy of the editorial chair of the *Critical Review*, caused it to be deservedly reprobated by those who admired justice and fair play, to say nothing of cultured criticism.

In one case, however, he was clearly in the right. A certain Admiral Knowles, who had so disgracefully failed in conducting to a successful issue the secret expedition to Rochelle in 1757, along with Sir John Mordaunt, wrote a pamphlet to justify his actions in the face of the storm of condemnation raised against him after a court–martial had acquitted Mordaunt. This pamphlet fell into Smollett's hands, who characterised the writer as 'an admiral without conduct, an engineer without knowledge, an officer without resolution, and a man without veracity.' Knowles entered an action against the printer, giving as his reason 'his desire to find out the writer, in order to obtain the satisfaction of a gentleman, if the writer's character would admit of it.' On Smollett learning this, he at once came forward, acknowledged himself as the writer, and declared his willingness to meet the admiral with any weapons he chose. But the latter was a poltroon and a coward. He had obtained a judgment of the Court, and he sheltered himself under it. Smollett was mulcted in £100, and in 1759 sentenced to three months' imprisonment. Knowles seems to have merited Sir Walter Scott's severe terms of reprobation: 'How the admiral reconciled his conduct to the rules usually observed by gentlemen we are not informed, but the proceedings seem to justify even Smollett's strength of expressions.'

But we have suffered our account of his relations to the *Critical Review* to run ahead of the narrative of his life. For several years the works he published were mostly hack–compilations for the booksellers. The most notable among these was *A Compendium of Authentic and Entertaining Voyages*, exhibiting a clear view of the Customs, Manners, Religion, Government, Commerce, and Natural History of most nations of the world, illustrated with a variety of Maps, Charts, etc., in 7 vols. 12mo. To this day Smollett's collection is read with appreciation, and only two years ago another edition (abridged) was published of this most interesting and instructive work.

Immense as was the reading and investigation required for such a compilation, Smollett cheerfully gave it, and really there are extraordinarily few errors in it notwithstanding the rapidity wherewith it had been produced. The publisher was Dodsley, and among the voyages recorded are those of Vasco da Gama, Pedro de Cabral, Magellan, Drake, Raleigh, Rowe, Monk, James, Nieuhoff, Wafer, Dampier, Gemelli, Rogers, Anson, etc., with the histories of the Conquest of Mexico and Peru. Also included therein was his own account of the expedition to Carthagena.

Some time before this Smollett had inserted in the *Critical Review* the following panegyric on Garrick, evidently intended to compensate for his bitter reflections on him in *Roderick Random* and *The Regicide*. Smollett's eyes were being opened to the more correct estimate of his own powers. Accordingly he wrote: 'We often see this inimitable actor labouring through five tedious acts to support a lifeless piece, with a mixture of pity and indignation, and cannot help wishing there were in his age good poets to write for one who so well deserves them. He has the art, like the Lydian king, of turning all he touches into gold, and can ensure applause to every fortunate bard.' Was the wish father to the deed? Be this as it may, within a short time Garrick accepted Smollett's comedy of *The Reprisal*, or *The Tars of Old England*, an afterpiece in two acts. The year 1757–58 had been a period of national disaster. Smollett, indignant at the timorous policy of the Government of the day, wrote the comedy in question to rouse the warlike spirit of the nation. The prologue begins—

'What eye will fail to glow, what eye to brighten,
When Britain's wrath aroused begins to lighten,
Her thunders roll—her fearless sons advance,
And her red ensigns wave o'er the pale flowers of France;

Her ancient splendour England shall maintain,
O'er distant realms extend her genial reign,
And rise the unrivall'd empress of the main.'

The Reprisal was performed at Drury Lane with great success, and Garrick's conduct on the occasion was generous in the extreme. It laid the foundations of a lifelong friendship between the two. The piece was afterwards published, and for some time held the stage as a 'curtain–raiser' or 'curtain–dropper,' but is now entirely forgotten.

At this period Smollet was on terms of intimate friendship with the famous John Wilkes, who has been often called 'the first Radical.' With Samuel Johnson also he had some friendly intercourse, though they were too alike to desire a great deal of intimate association with each other. Smollett, however, through his influence with Wilkes, was able to obtain the release of Dr. Johnson's black servant, Francis Barber, who had been impressed and put on board the *Stag* frigate. On the occasion Smollett wrote to Wilkes in the following terms:—

'CHELSEA, *March 16, 1759.*

'I am again your petitioner in behalf of that Great Cham of literature, Samuel Johnson. His black servant, whose name is Francis Barber, has been pressed on board the *Stag* frigate, Captain Angel, and our lexicographer is in great distress. He says the boy is a sickly lad of a delicate frame, and particularly subject to a malady in the throat, which renders him very unfit for His Majesty's service. You know what manner of animosity the said Johnson has against you, and I daresay you desire no other opportunity of resenting it than that of laying him under an obligation.'

The application was successful, and Francis Barber returned to the lexicographer's service. Dr. Johnson always spoke of Dr. Smollett thereafter with great respect:—'A scholarly man, sir, although a Scot.'

CHAPTER VIII

HISTORY OF ENGLAND—SIR LAUNCELOT GREAVES—THE NORTH BRITON—HACK HISTORICAL WORK—THE BEGINNING OF THE END.

Despite all his hastiness of temper and irritability, despite his wife's lack of management, despite, too, the fact of the burden of debt weighing him down, the Chelsea home must have been a very happy one. At this time Smollett had one child, a daughter, Elizabeth, to whom he was tenderly attached. Nothing rejoiced him more than a frolic with his little one. 'Many a time,' he remarks in one of his unpublished letters, now in the possession of Mr. Goring, 'do I stop my task and betake me to a game of romps with Betty, while my wife looks on smiling and longing in her heart to join in the sport: then back to the cursed round of duty.'

Mrs. Smollett appears to have been of a most affectionate and loving disposition, though, like himself, she was affected with a hasty temper. Though they had many quarrels, they were deeply and sincerely attached to each other. 'My Nancy' appears in many of his letters in conjunction with expressions of the tenderest and truest affection. The home was always bright and cheerful for the weary worker, hence, when absent from it, he is ever craving 'to be back to Nancy and little Bet' Yet these were feelings Smollett scrupulously concealed from his fellows, so that the world might suppose him the acidulous cynic he desired to be esteemed. What Smollett's reason for so acting was, is now hard to divine. His Matthew Bramble in *Humphrey Clinker* is the exact reproduction of his own character. His kindliness of nature only broke out like gleams of sunshine on a wintry day, while, like Jonathan Oldbuck, the very suggestion of gratitude seemed to irritate him. He was one who all his life preferred to do good by stealth.

In 1758, Smollett published a work that had occupied his attention throughout the better part of eighteen months—*The Complete History of England, deduced from the descent of Julius Cæsar to the Treaty of Aix–la–Chapelle in 1748*. It was published by Messrs. Rivington & Fletcher, in four vols. 4to, and embellished by engraved allegorical frontispieces, designed by Messrs. Hayman & Miller. It has been stated, and never contradicted, says Anderson (substantiated also by Herbert), that the history was written in fourteen months, an effort to which nothing but the most distinguished abilities and the most vigorous application could have been equal. When one considers that he consulted three hundred books for information, that he had other literary work to prosecute in order to keep the pot boiling, and when one has regard also to the high literary character of the composition, this rapidity of production is simply marvellous. Of course none of the facts were new, but the method was novel, and the treatment fresh and brilliant. As Sir Walter Scott justly remarks, 'All the novelty which Smollett's history could present, must needs consist in the mode of stating facts, or in the reflections deduced from them.' The success which attended the publication of the history surpassed the expectations of even Smollett himself. His political standpoint had been that of a Tory and an upholder of the monarchy. In writing to Dr. Moore early in 1758, Smollett says: 'I deferred answering your kind letter until I should have finished my History, which is now completed. I was agreeably surprised to hear that my work had met with any approbation in Glasgow, for it is not at all calculated for that meridian. The last volume will, I doubt not, be severely censured by the West Country Whigs of Scotland. I desire you will divest yourself of prejudice before you begin to peruse it, and consider well the facts before you pass judgment. Whatever may be its defect, I profess before God I have, as far as in me lay, adhered to truth, without espousing any faction.' Then in September of the same year he again writes to Dr. Moore: 'You will not be sorry to hear that the weekly sale of the History has increased to above 10,000. A French gentleman of talents and erudition has undertaken to translate it into that language, and I have promised to supply him with corrections.'

But sadder and still more sad grows the picture of distress. During the whole time he was writing his History he was pestered by duns, and could not leave his home without dodging bailiffs. When all was over, he found himself a man broken in health and spirits, and already 'earmarked' for the tomb. For fourteen years he was to live and labour, like the brave, honest, independent spirit he was, but the end was only a question of time. That he realised this fact about this period is almost certain. Henceforth his diligence was redoubled. Like the stranger from another world in the fable, when confronted with the fact of inevitable death, he cried, 'I must die, I must die; trouble me not with trifles; I must die.'

But his publication of the History was not suffered to pass without the formation of another party bent on injuring him. The extensive sale of Smollett's work alarmed the proprietors of Rapin's History, who caballed and encouraged his political adversaries to expose what they termed 'the absurdities, inconsistencies, contradictions, and misrepresentations of the book,' most of which existed solely in the minds of his malignant enemies. In the Whig periodicals of the time Smollett is vilified and abused, represented as a partisan and panegyrist of the House of Stuart, a Papist and a prostitute. The following pamphlet, written, however, by a man of some learning and discernment, would have been valuable and useful had it only been penned with more moderation and good sense. But party zeal is an enemy to good sense, and the truth of this remark has seldom been more clearly demonstrated than in '*A Vindication of the Revolution in 1688*, and of the character of King William and Queen Mary, together with a computation of the character of King James II., as misrepresented by the author of the Complete History of England, by extracts from Dr. Smollett: to which are added some strictures on the said historian's account of the punishment of the rebels in A.D. 1715 and 1746, and on the eulogium given to the History of England by the critical reviewers, by Thomas Comber, B.A. 8vo, 1758.' Comber was a clergyman, and a relative of the Duke of Leeds. He was, in fact, engaged by the Whig Ministry to undertake the duty, as none of the professed *litterateurs* of the day in the Whig ranks cared to cross swords with the Tory champion in his own field. The publication of his History did Smollett much good in the eyes of the learned and cultured. Henceforth to them he was no longer a mere 'teller of tales,' but one of the great historians of the epoch—an author deservedly honoured for his integrity and impartiality.

In 1761 the *British Magazine*—a sixpenny monthly on whose staff Oliver Goldsmith was one of the leading writers—published *The Adventures of Sir Launcelot Greaves*, the fourth of Smollett's novels, but the one which we could quite well have spared, provided something in the same vein as *Humphrey Clinker* had taken its place. It was written hastily, and to supply the demand for *copy*. Scott relates that, while engaged on it, he was residing at Paxton in Berwickshire, on a visit to Mr. George Home. When post time drew near, he was wont to retire for half an hour or an hour, and then and there scribble off the necessary amount of matter for the press. But he never gave himself even the trouble to read over and correct what he had written. Work written under such circumstances did not deserve to succeed. And yet, singularly enough, in this novel are to be found some of Smollett's most original creations and most felicitously conceived situations. The design of the work is far from happy. Obviously suggested by his recent study of *Don Quixote*, Sir Launcelot is only a bad imitation of the immortal Knight of La Mancha. Of this, indeed, Smollett himself seems to have had a suspicion. In the course of the dialogue he makes Ferret express an opinion like that to Sir Launcelot, who sternly repudiates it. 'What! you set up for a modern Don Quixote? The scheme is too stale and extravagant. What was a humorous and well–timed satire in Spain near two hundred years ago will make but a sorry jest when really acted from affectation at this time of day in England.' The knight, eyeing the censor, whose character was none of the best, replied, 'I am neither an affected imitation of Don Quixote, nor, as I trust in Heaven, visited by that spirit of lunacy so admirably displayed in the fictitious character exhibited by the inimitable Cervantes. I see and distinguish objects as they are seen and described by other men. I quarrel with none but the foes of virtue and decorum, against whom I have declared perpetual war, and them I will everywhere attack as the natural enemies of mankind. I do purpose,' added Sir Launcelot, eyeing Ferret with a look of ineffable contempt, 'to act as a coadjutor to the law, and even to remedy evils which the law cannot reach, to detect fraud and treason, abase insolence, mortify pride, discourage slander, disgrace immodesty, stigmatise ingratitude.'

The work was written in part during his imprisonment. Taking this into consideration, as well as the rapidity of production, the conception, amid the sordid surroundings of the King's Bench Prison, of such cleverly drawn characters as Aurelia Darnel, Captain Crowe, and his nephew, Tom Clarke, the attorney of the amorous heart, is passing wonderful. Although the least popular of his works, and deservedly so, the book in some parts is redolent of 'Flora and the country green.'

Not a moment could his busy pen afford to rest. No sooner was one piece of work thrown off than another must be commenced. In 1761, Smollett lent his assistance to the furtherance of a great work. This was the publication, in 42 vols. 8vo, of *The Modern Part of an Universal History, compiled from Original Writers.* In this colossal undertaking we know that Smollett's share was the Histories of France, Italy, and Germany. Not alone these, however, were the fruit of his industry. Other authors failed to produce their quota. There was one pen that never failed. The willing horse had to do the work. Though this additional labour brought in guineas, it still further exhausted his strength, and left him little better than a confirmed invalid. From this drudgery he passed on to something else that was a little more agreeable and congenial, namely, his *Continuation of the History of England.* The first volume was published in the end of 1761, the second, third, and fourth in 1762, and a fifth some years after (1765), bringing the narrative down to that period. It is stated that Smollett cleared £2000 by his History and the Continuation. He sold the latter to his printer at a price which enabled the purchaser to sell it to Mr. Baldwin the bookseller at a profit of £1000. From these facts one can gather the extraordinary popularity of Smollett's work at that period.

Henceforward the story of his life is summed up in little more than the dates of the publication of his books. Of relaxation there was no interval for him. His expenses of living were considerable, though he never was a man who loved luxury or display. But he had been hampered by debts, by lawsuits, to pay the costs of which he had to borrow money at sixty per cent. Had Smollett's feet been free from the outset, the £600 per annum, at which he reckoned his income, would have more than sufficed for all his wants. But the interest of borrowed money is like the rolling snowball of which we spoke before,—unless it be paid regularly, it constantly adds to the bulk of the original. Poor Smollett! A more pitiable picture can scarcely be conceived than this splendid genius yoked like a pug–mill horse to tasks the most ignoble, in order that he might keep his wife and daughter from feeling the pinch of want. A hero—yea, a hero indeed—one of those heroes in commonplace things, whose virtues are every whit as praiseworthy in their way as though he had led England's armies to victory, or swept the seas of her enemies.

In connection with Smollett's historical work, it should be mentioned here, that although his History has not held its place as a standard work, his Continuation undoubtedly has. To this day it is printed along with Hume's volumes, under the title of *Hume and Smollett's History of England*, and is justly held in esteem for its impartiality and accuracy. His other historical works have long since met the fate they deserved. They were hack–work, designed to supply a temporary need. When that need was met by something better, they were forgotten.

We must note here, however, in disproof of that jealousy of contemporaries which has been laid to his charge, the following generous estimate of those who were his *collaborateurs* in some respects, his rivals in others. In the Continuation he thus repairs the hasty judgments of immature years: 'Akenside and Armstrong excelled in didactic poetry. Candidates for literary fame appeared even in the higher sphere of life, embellished by the nervous style, superior sense, and extensive erudition of a Coke, by the delicate taste, the polished muse, and tender feelings of a Lyttleton. There are also the learned and elegant Robertson, and, above all, the ingenious, penetrating, and comprehensive Hume, whom we rank among the first writers of the age, both as a historian and a philosopher. Johnson, inferior to none in philosophy, philology, poetry, and classical learning, stands foremost as an essayist, justly admired for the dignity, strength, and variety of his style, as well as for the agreeable manner in which he investigates the human heart, tracing every interesting emotion, and opening all the sources of morality!' And this was the man whom his political opponents accused of never speaking of a man save to depreciate him.

We reach now a period in Smollett's career which must always give pain to those that are lovers of his genius. Hitherto, though dabbling in politics, and though editing, professedly on the Tory and High Church side, the *Critical Review*, his sympathies had been so predominatingly literary that he was able to maintain the friendliest of relations with prominent politicians on the Whig side, notably with John Wilkes. Now, in an evil hour, he was prevailed upon to accept a brief on the Tory side by assuming the editorship of the new weekly paper, *The Briton*, founded for the express purpose of defending the Earl of Bute. That nobleman, who owed his advancement to the favour wherewith he was regarded by George III.(recently come to the throne), was, on the 29th May 1762, appointed First Lord of the Treasury, and assumed the management of public affairs. Although an able, honourable, and indefatigable Minister, he lacked experience in the discharge of public duties. Besides, the nation was still strongly Whig in its political inclinations. For the monarch, by an arbitrary exercise of his prerogative, thus to override the sentiments of his people and to dismiss their chosen representatives, was both a high–handed and a foolish action. More foolish still was Lord Bute that he permitted himself thus to be made a tool to gratify the king's jealousy. The consequence was, that the appointment was received all over England with a storm of indignation, and no Ministry was ever more unpopular than that whereof the Earl of Bute was chief.

To stem the tide of adverse criticism, and endeavour to win Englishmen to view more favourably the advent of Lord Bute to power, *The Briton* was started, and Smollett was chosen as editor, inasmuch as his was the keenest pen on the Tory side. On hearing of the appointment of his friend to the post, John Wilkes, with a generosity that was quite in keeping with many of the actions of that strangely constituted man, remarked that 'Lord Bute, after having distributed among his adherents all the places under Government, was determined to monopolise the wit also.' A few days subsequent, the Whigs proposed that, to encounter *The Briton*, which had gone off with a great flourish of trumpets, as well as with some very bitter political writing, Mr. Wilkes should publish a paper, to be called 'The Englishman.' He agreed to the proposal, except that he did not adopt the title recommended, but chose another, that of *The North Briton*—the first number of which appeared on the 5th June 1762, or exactly a week after *The Briton*.

Wilkes exhibited great forbearance towards Smollett at the outset. The good–natured demagogue, it is believed, would have been content, like many another pair of friends, to fight strenuously for principles, and avoid personalities; or, if that were impossible, to confine their antagonism to the press alone, leaving the intercourse of friendship unimpaired. But Smollett was not of the stuff whereof great journalists are made. One of the prime qualities is that they should belong to the genus of literary pachydermata. Smollett was not so. He was sensitive to a degree. He imagined slights and insults where none were intended. Within a few days, therefore, of the issue of *The North Briton*, Smollett took umbrage at something said about *The Briton*, and retorted angrily with some personalities on Wilkes. Even then the latter would have passed over the ill–natured jibes with a jest. This, however, maddened Smollett more than aught else. He believed Wilkes despised him as an assailant. From that day Smollett devoted himself to the most unsparing personal castigation of Wilkes. The demagogue replied, and presently the two that had been such warm friends could not find terms bitter enough to hurl at one another.

But Smollett was not a match for Wilkes. The former was scrupulously careful in alleging nothing against his opponent but what he could prove. The latter fought with characteristic unscrupulousness. A matter of no moment to him was it whether a charge were true or false, provided it served the purpose of galling his adversary. Wilkes was absolutely impervious to abuse and vilification. He gloried in his indifference to all social restrictions and customs. The publication to the world of his debaucheries and lack of principle only extorted a horse–laugh from him. With all his generosity and faithful devotion to the cause of popular freedom, Wilkes was a man of absolutely no principle. He sneered at his family relations, was one of Sir Francis Dashwood's Medmenham 'Cistercians,' who sought to outbid the 'Hellfire' and 'Devil's Own' Clubs in abandoned wickedness and impiety. And yet this was the man who was capable of the most splendid sacrifice in the cause of national liberty. His abilities would have carried him to fame in any career. M. Louis Blanc states that many of his sayings are still repeated and admired in France as are those of Sydney Smith among us. Mr. J. Bowles Daly[8] relates that his wit was so constantly at his command, that wagers have been gained that from the time he quitted his house till he reached Guildhall, no one could address him or leave him without a smile or a hearty laugh. His bright conversation charmed away the prejudice of such a Tory as Dr. Johnson, fascinated Hannah More, and won over the gloomy Lord Mansfield, who said, 'Mr. Wilkes is the pleasantest companion, the politest gentleman, and the best scholar I know.'

This, then, was the man who was selected to do battle with Smollett and to demolish the Ministry of Lord Bute. Certainly the latter had given Wilkes ample handle for assailing him by selecting as his Chancellor of the Exchequer Lord Sandwich, one of the dissolute Medmenham monks, a man glaringly deficient in ability, and so utterly incompetent in finance as to cause the wits of the time to describe him as 'a Chancellor of the Exchequer to whom a sum of five figures was an impenetrable mystery.' The first sentence of *The North Briton* has often been copied and adopted as the motto of succeeding journals: 'The liberty of the press is the birthright of the Briton, and is justly esteemed the firmest bulwark of the liberties of this country.' The aim of Wilkes' paper was to vilify Scotland, because Lord Bute, being a Scotsman, had wormed himself into the favour of the king. Not a very elevated principle, certainly, but quite characteristic of the low *morale* of the period, when personal pique was elevated into the domain of principle. His abuse of Scotland was quite of a piece with his political profligacy on every other point than national liberty. 'He would have sold his soul to the devil for £1000 could he have induced his Satanic majesty to have invested in so worthless a commodity,' said one of his own friends. As a specimen of the journalism wherewith Wilkes fought the battle of popular liberties, take the following paragraph, to pen which nowadays not the neediest penny–a–liner of gutter–journalism would stoop, notwithstanding the jealousy of Scotland and the Scots which still exists. Playing on the popular jealousy of Scotland, Wilkes went on to say that 'The river Tweed is the line of demarcation between all that is noble and all that is base; south of the river is all honour, virtue, patriotism—north of it is nothing but lying, malice, meanness, and slavery. Scotland is a treeless, flowerless land, formed out of the refuse of the universe, and inhabited by the very bastards of creation; where famine has fixed her chosen throne; where a scant population, gaunt with hunger and hideous with dirt, spend their wretched days in brooding over the fallen fortunes of their native dynasty, and in watching with mingled envy and hatred the mighty nation that subdued them.'

This was the type of writing which Smollett strove to meet with pithy argument and epigrammatic smartness. No wonder it produced little effect, and less wonder is there that, after fighting the battle of the Ministry for nearly a year, he threw the task up in disgust (12th February 1763). Lord Bute had not given him the support he had a right to expect; and the Minister's own fall followed hard upon the cessation of *The Briton*, namely, on the 8th April of the same year. Writing to Caleb Whiteford, a friend, some time after, he remarked: 'The Ministry little deserve that any man of genius should draw his pen in their defence. They inherit the absurd stoicism of Lord Bute, who set himself up as a pillory to be pelted by all the blackguards of England, upon the supposition that they would grow tired and leave off.'

Back once more to hack–work was our weary, brain–worn veteran. So pressing were his needs that he had to condescend to tasks beneath them. He translated and edited the works of Voltaire, and compiled a publication entitled *The Present State of all Nations*, containing a geographical, natural, commercial, and political history of all the countries of the known world. Fancy Smollett engaged on such a task! Let us hope that only his name was given, not his labour. Next year we know his work became so great that he had to hire others to do portions of it for him. In a word, he became a literary 'sweater.'

Alas! in this same year, 1763, when his own health was failing so rapidly, one of the links binding him most strongly to earth was severed. His daughter Elizabeth, a beautiful girl of some fifteen or sixteen years of age, and amiable and accomplished as well, was taken from him by death—the saddest of all deaths, consumption. Henceforth he was to tread the Valley of the Shadow alone. Even more than his wife, Elizabeth had been able to sympathise with her father's feelings and to soothe his irritation. The light of his life had verily gone out!

But still no rest! Sorrow, however deep, must not check the pen that is fighting for daily bread. 'I am writing with a breaking heart,' he says in one letter. 'I would wish to be beside her, were the wish not cowardly so long as poor Nancy is unprovided for.' Brave, suffering heart! The end is nearing for you, though you know it not. Seven more years of increasing labour, and also of increasing anguish and suffering, and then—'He giveth His beloved sleep!'

CHAPTER IX

SMOLLETT A 'SWEATER'—TRAVELS ABROAD—*THE ADVENTURES OF AN ATOM—HUMPHREY CLINKER*—LAST DAYS.

So deeply did grief over the death of his charming young daughter prey on his health and spirits, that there were for a time grave doubts whether his reason had not been slightly unsettled. Constitutionally of a nervously sensitive nature, excessive joy or sorrow had a thoroughly unhinging effect upon him. He had not the self–command requisite to look upon grief as one of those ills to which flesh is heir. In his estimation, everything affecting himself was in the superlative degree. Never were sorrows so overwhelming as his, he considered, and oftentimes he seriously mortified people by brusquely breaking in upon their anguish with the statement that they did not really know what grief meant in comparison with him.

After Elizabeth's death, therefore, Smollett, entirely oblivious of his poor wife's mental sufferings, seems to have abandoned himself to an excess of grief that seriously accelerated the progress of the maladies by which he was afflicted. Though he could not afford to stop work altogether, he appears from this date to have instituted a sort of literary factory, where works were turned out by the score. Smollett's name was now so popular, that on a title–page it virtually meant success to the publication. He therefore contracted the habit of undertaking far more work than any man single–handed could accomplish, but getting it executed at a reduced rate by those whom he retained in his employment. He appears to have kept them in food and clothing, and to have been in the main exceedingly kind to many a struggling author, who would not otherwise have obtained employment; but one cannot approve of methods like these, which degrade the noble profession of 'man of letters' into that of a literary task–master. Dr. Carlyle gives a description of Smollett's relations to what 'Jupiter' called his 'myrmidons,' which, however, affords a somewhat one–sided picture of the novelist's methods, though the date is scarcely correct. Smollett, although he had employed others to do his work for him when he found it to be too onerous, did not really institute his 'literary factory' until well on in the 'sixties' of the eighteenth century, when his health was beginning to fail. 'Jupiter' describes the 'factory' as in full swing in 1758–59. But as the chatty old clerical gossip wrote his Autobiography after his seventy–ninth year, and as many of his dates with respect to other matters have been proved incorrect, we may, without much injustice to the best of Scots unepiscopal bishops, ascribe to the mental feebleness of age an error which otherwise would affix a serious stigma on Smollett's name. Though every *litterateur* worth the name will reprobate such a blood–sucking method as literary 'sweating,' prosecuted though it has been by men to whom we owe so much as Smollett and Dumas (to say nothing of at least one 'popular' author in our own day who engages in the despicable practice), we would fain believe, in the former's case, that it resulted from failing strength, and from the maddening consciousness of being obliged to leave his wife, if he died, dependent on strangers.

But let us to 'Jupiter':[9] 'Principal Robertson had never met Smollett (though he had seen him at the Select Club), and was very desirous of his acquaintance. By this time the Doctor had retired to Chelsea, and came seldom to town. Home and I, however, found that he came once a week to Forrest's Coffee–house, and sometimes dined there; so we managed an appointment with him on his day, when he agreed to dine with us. He was now become a great man, and, being a humorist, was not to be put out of his way. Home and Robertson and Smith and I met him there, when he had several of his minions about him, to whom he prescribed tasks of translation, compilation, or abridgment, which, after he had seen, he recommended to the booksellers. We dined together, and Smollett was very brilliant. Having to stay all night, that we might spend the evening together, he only begged leave to withdraw for an hour, that he might give audience to his myrmidons. We insisted that if his business permitted, it should be in the room in which we sat. The Doctor agreed, and the authors were introduced, to the number of five, I think, most of whom were soon dismissed. He kept two, however, to supper, whispering to us that he believed they would amuse us, which they certainly did, for they were curious characters. We passed a very pleasant and joyful evening. When we broke up, Robertson expressed great surprise at Smollett's polished and agreeable manners, and the great urbanity of his conversation. He had imagined that a man's manners must bear a likeness to his books, and as Smollett had described so well the characters of ruffians and profligates, that he must of course resemble them.'

In addition to the pitiful lack of taste and good feeling in making a raree–show of wretchedness, and holding up the misery of the unfortunate authors to a curiosity that was worse than contempt, the whole incident exhibits the characters of Smollett, Carlyle, Robertson, and Home in an exceedingly unfavourable aspect—the first–named as glorifying himself as the Mæcenas of starving Grub Street quill–drivers, the others because they could entertain any other feeling than that of sympathy for honest talent in tatters!

In June 1763, Smollett's health and spirits became alike so unsatisfactory that his medical adviser informed Mrs. Smollett that change of air was the only chance for him. His sorrow was preying on his vitality. As that was low enough at any time, the prospect was grave indeed! Alas, poor Nancy! She pled with her obdurate husband for many a week before he consented to wind up his numberless projects in England and go abroad. His creditors also seem to have behaved with commendable consideration. Perhaps the fact that a small legacy of £1200 left to Mrs. Smollett by one of her relatives, and which, with true wifelike generosity, she at once applied to the relief of her unfortunate husband, may have facilitated matters. That he left England with arrangements made whereby his 'myrmidons' were to forward their 'copy' to him, whithersoever he might be, goes without the saying. The booksellers, also—Newbery, Baldwin, Dodsley, Cave (jr.), and others—all exhibited a willingness to assist the man who had done so much for them. But therein they did no more than their duty.

For nearly three years Smollett and his wife remained abroad, travelling in France and Italy, but allocating a portion of every day to the discharge of those tasks which kept the chariot rolling. When he returned to England in 1766, he published, as the fruit of his trip, *Travels through France and Italy: containing Observations on Character, Customs, Religion, Government, Police, Commerce, Arts, Antiquities, with a Particular Description of the Town, Territory, and Climate of Nice; to which is added a Register of the Weather, kept during a Residence of Eighteen Months there.* In 2 vols. 8vo. The book takes the form of letters written by Smollett to friends at home; and in the first letter he remarks: 'In gratifying your curiosity I shall find some amusement to beguile the tedious hours, which without some employment would be rendered insupportable by distemper and disquiet.' The spirit wherein Smollett went on tour is perceptible in the following passage: 'I am traduced by malice, persecuted by faction, and overwhelmed by the sense of a domestic calamity which it was not in the power of fortune to repair.'

Travelling and brooding do not accord well together, if one is to receive any pleasure from the scenes passed through. As Dr. Anderson charitably puts it: 'His letters afford a melancholy proof of the influence of bodily pain over the best disposition.' Letters written under such circumstances should never have been published. In the exquisite scenery through which he passed, in the objects of interest in the galleries and museums, he appears only to have discovered subjects whereupon his bitter, acidulous humour could expend itself. Dr. Moore well observes: 'Those who are disgusted with such descriptions are not the only people to whom Smollett gave offence: he exposed himself also to the reprehension of the whole class of connoisseurs, the real as well as the far more numerous body of pretenders to that science. For example, what is one to think of a man who likened the snow–clad glories of the Alps to frosted sugar; who said of the famous Venus de Medicis, that has awakened the admiration of ages, "I cannot help thinking there is no beauty in the features of Venus, and that the attitude is awkward and out of character"; and who remarked of the Pantheon, "I was much disappointed at sight of the Pantheon, which, after all that has been said of it, looks like a huge cockpit open at the top"?'

The chastisement came, but from the one man who, of all others, should have remained silent—a man whose whole life was a pitiful epitome of those faults he sought to reprehend in Smollett—Laurence Sterne. Jealousy, of course, was the motive. The author of *Tristram Shandy* could never forgive the fact that the public preferred *Peregrine Pickle* to the prurient puerilities of Uncle Toby. Sterne did not take into consideration, moreover, the state of Smollett's health, and how it would colour every estimate he formed of men, manners, and things. The last in the world was the author of *Tristram Shandy* to have sat as moral or æsthetic critic on Smollett. How the mighty sledge–hammer of contempt wielded by Sir Walter Scott crushed the unfeeling, though far from radically ill–natured critic! Sterne wrote: 'The learned Smelfungus travelled from Boulogne to Paris, from Paris to Rome, and so on, but he set out with the spleen and the jaundice, and every object he passed by was discoloured and distorted. He wrote an account of them, but it was nothing but an account of his miserable feelings. I met Smelfungus in the grand portico of the Pantheon. He was just coming out of it. "It is nothing but a huge cockpit," said he. "I wish you had said nothing worse of the Venus Medicis," replied I—for in passing through Florence I had heard he had fallen foul upon the goddess, and used her worse than a common strumpet, without the least provocation in nature. I popped upon Smelfungus again in Turin, in his return home, and a sad tale of sorrowful adventures he had to tell, wherein he spoke of "moving accidents by flood and field, and of the cannibals which each other eat, the Anthropophagi." He had been flayed alive and bedeviled, and worse used than Saint Bartholomew at every stage he had come at. "I'll tell it," said Smelfungus, "to the world." "You had better tell it," said I, "to your physician."' Now, though Smollett deserved castigation for inflicting his miseries on the public and ridiculing many of their most cherished ideals at a time when he was mentally unfit to judge, the passage cited above is not the manner in which such literary punishment should be given. Thereupon says Sir Walter: 'Be it said without offence to the memory of that witty and elegant writer (Sterne), it is more easy to assume in composition an air of alternate gaiety and sensibility, than to practise the virtues of generosity and benevolence which Smollett exercised during his whole life, though often, like his own Matthew Bramble, under the disguise of peevishness and irritability. Sterne's writings show much flourish concerning virtues of which his life is understood to have produced little fruit; the temper of Smollett was—

"Like a lusty winter,
Frosty, but kindly."'

Alas! not long now was the worn tenement of the great novelist to hold his fiery spirit. After 1766 the end was known to be only a question of a year or two at most. Manfully and nobly did he receive the intelligence. There was no repining at the hardness of his lot. 'My poor Nancy; let me make the best use of the time for her.' Constant rheumatism, and the pain arising from a neglected ulcer which had developed into a chronic sore, had so drained his strength that there was no recovering the lost ground. A premature break–up of the system, rather than the positive disease of consumption, numbered his days.

Soon after returning home from the Continent, he repaired to Scotland to visit his aged mother. Affecting in the last degree was that visit. To both the knowledge was present that never more on earth would they meet. The old lady, with that keen insight into the future which often distinguishes the aged, said, 'We'll no' be long parted, any way. If you go first, I'll be close on your heels: if I lead the way, ye'll no' be far behind me, I'm thinking.' And so it proved. Though in Scotland he enjoyed a partial restoration to health that cheered some of his friends, his mother knew better. 'The last flicker of the candle is aye the brightest,' she said. While in Scotland he visited, with his sister Mrs. Telfer and his biographer Dr. Moore, the Smolletts of Bonhill, where he received a warm welcome from his cousin, who pressed him to stay there for some months and get his health thoroughly established.

But the treadmill in London was waiting for its victim. In the beginning of 1767 he returned to London, having sojourned at Bath for a time with Mrs. Smollett. Once more he was back tugging at the oar, doing odd work for the *Critical Review*, compiling travels, translating from French, Spanish, or Latin sundry books of merely ephemeral interest. Then he contributed to the periodical literature of the day—anything, in fact, to keep that wolf from the door which every year seemed to approach nearer and yet nearer.

Only two more works of any moment was he to live to accomplish—one, an indifferent production judged by his own high standard—the other, like the dying cygnet's song in Grecian fable—the greatest and the last! In 1769 appeared *The History and Adventures of an Atom*, in 2 vols. 12mo. This is a politico–social satire, wherein are represented the several leaders of political parties from 1754 till the dissolution of Lord Chatham's administration in 1762, but under the thin veil of Japanese names. George III. was consumed with the fallacy that he was the first statesman in the Europe of his day. His experiments in diplomacy nearly brought Britain to ruin. Had he not bullied and badgered the elder Pitt into resignation, America would have been to–day an integral part of the Empire, which would have feared no rival from pole to pole. But such was not to be. Besides, out of the blundering of the honest but short–sighted monarch the liberties of the English people were to be evolved. *The History of an Atom* was successful, but is to–day the portion of Smollett's writings with which we could most comfortably dispense. It is a satire, or intended for such, but accommodates itself to none of the known rules of any school of satiric writing. Neither to Swift, Arbuthnot, Steele, nor Butler does it exhibit affinity.

Towards the middle of 1768 the fact became evident to all, that if Smollett's life was to be preserved, he must henceforth live far from the bitter winters of England. To leave his fatherland he was not sorry. Faction had embittered his existence during the past few years, and faction was jealously to pursue him with its malice even to the end. His only political friends neglected him who had fought so well and indefatigably for them. The Earl of Bute with but little exertion could have placed Smollett at once beyond the necessity of such killing labour. But the Butes, then, were proverbially notorious for their callousness and their ingratitude.

When the final verdict was given, Smollett endeavoured to obtain some consulship abroad, that would have lessened his labours. He was still dependent on his pen for daily bread. Almost despairingly he implored even his political enemies to help him to some means whereby he might demit some portion of his killing work. But his 'noble' friends were all deaf. Lord Shelburne was applied to, but stated the consulships at Nice and Leghorn were already promised to some of his own political creatures. One man only stood his friend; one man only, and he an opponent albeit a countryman, did his best for Smollett, but, alas! unavailingly. All honour to David Hume the historian, then Under Secretary of State! In the end the dying novelist was disappointed at all points. He had to go abroad depending on the staff that had supplied him with bread all through the long years until now—and which alone would not now fail him—his pen!

Smollett left England in December 1768, and proceeded to Leghorn *via* Lucca and Pisa. Here he settled at Monte Nova, a little township situated on the side of a mountain overlooking the sea. Dr. Armstrong, his friend and countryman, had secured for him a beautiful villa on the outskirts of the village. Here he gradually grew weaker, but was tended with the utmost devotion by his wife, and some of the English families in the neighbourhood. Here, too, he penned the greatest of his novels, the work that for its subtle insight into human nature, its keen and incisive studies of character, its delightful humour, its matchless *bonhomie* and raciness, takes rank amidst the treasured classics of our literature—the immortal *Humphrey Clinker.*

But with this exertion the feeble flame of the great novelist's life slowly flickered out. His work was done, and nobly done. He had carved for himself an imperishable niche in the great Temple of Fame. His last words were spoken to his wife—'All is well, my dear;' and on the 21st October 1771, in the 52nd year of his age, Tobias George Smollett laid down the burden of that life which had pressed so wearily upon him, and passed—within the Silence!

He had the pleasure of seeing *Humphrey Clinker* in its published form a day or two before his death. When the public learned that the hand which so often had delighted them in the past would now delight them no more, a mournful interest was exhibited in his last work. Edition after edition was exhausted. But what booted it to him, then, when the strife and the anguish as well as the exultation born of success were all over? 'After labour cometh rest, and after strife the guerdon.' Alas! too late the latter came to cheer him whose life had been one long–drawn–out epic of anguish from the cradle to the grave!

Had Smollett lived four years longer, he would have inherited the estate of Bonhill and an income of £1000 per annum, which in default of him passed to Mrs. Telfer, his sister, and her heirs. O the irony of fate! Alas! the thorn of apprehension which disturbed his dying pillow proved too true a dread. His wife was left in Leghorn in dire penury, until relieved by the charity of friends who were *not* relatives, and also by the proceeds of a theatrical performance given in her aid after some years by Mr. Graham of Gartmore. An indelible stain is it upon the Telfers and the Smolletts that they should have allowed the widow of their most distinguished relative to die dependent on the charity of strangers. But relatives are proverbially the hardest–hearted of potential benefactors when the day of trouble comes. Poor "Narcissa"! the lines of her life were not cast in pleasant places.

Smollett was interred in the English cemetery at Leghorn, with the blue Mediterranean stretching in front of his last resting–place. Many are the pilgrims that journey to his tomb, and as the years roll on they increase rather than diminish. A plain monument was erected by his wife over the remains, the Latin inscription on which was written by his friend Dr. Armstrong, the poet. At Bonhill, a splendid obelisk, over sixty feet high, was raised on the banks of the Leven, by his cousin James Smollett (a few months before his own death), the inscription being revised and corrected by Dr. Johnson.

Dr. Moore, as the friend of Smollett, has preserved for us the appearance and portrait of the great novelist in the following description: "The person of Dr. Smollett was stout and well proportioned, his countenance engaging, his manner reserved, with a certain air of dignity that seemed to indicate that he was not unconscious of his own powers. He was of a disposition so humane and generous that he was ever ready to serve the unfortunate, and on some occasions to assist them beyond what his circumstances could justify. Though few could penetrate with more acuteness into character, yet none was more apt to overlook misconduct when attended by misfortune. Free from vanity, Smollett had a considerable share of pride and great sensibility; his passions were easily moved, and too impetuous when roused. He could not conceal his contempt of folly, his detestation of fraud, nor refrain from proclaiming his indignation against every instance of oppression. He was of an intrepid, independent, imprudent disposition, equally incapable of deceit and adulation, and more disposed to cultivate the acquaintance of those he could serve than of those who could serve him."

Such being the character of the man, the key is obtained to the enigma of Smollet's lack of political and social success. He was of too honest a nature to do the dirty work of the 'Ministers' of the time, amongst whom independence of character was rated as a sin of the first magnitude. But in the hearts of the admirers of his literary works, Smollett will also live as one of the greatest of our countrymen—a man whose virtues are yearly becoming recognised in their true light, as readers realise he is one of the world's great moral teachers, whose lessons are communicated by exhibiting the naked hideousness of vice. And so the star of his fame will shine more and yet more clearly unto the perfect day!

CHAPTER X

SMOLLETT AS A NOVELIST

Smollett, although gaining distinction in other branches of literature, was primarily and essentially a novelist. He wrote history, and wrote it well; drama, and wrote it only passably; travels but little better, and poetry decidedly mechanically, save in the 'Ode to Independence.' In the novel alone did he by prescriptive right take his place in the front rank of British writers of fiction. Wherein then lay his strength, and in what respects did he differ from Richardson and Fielding? To institute any comparative estimate between the three is foolish in the last degree. The grounds for such a comparison do not exist, save in the initial fact that all three wrote novels!

Smollett was, like Scott, an unequalled observer. Nothing missed his 'inevitable eye,' either in a situation, an incident, or a landscape. If he had not Fielding's keen power of vision into the mental and moral characteristics of his fellow–men, he had twice his aptness of objective photography. The ludicrous aspects of a circumstance or of a saying impressed him deeply. He never seemed to forget the humorous bearings of any experience through which he had passed, or of which he had learned. The *affaire de cœur* with Melinda in *Roderick Random*, the challenge and arrest through the affection of Strap, also the inimitable 'banquet after the manner of the ancients' in *Peregrine Pickle*, were described from incidents occurring in Smollett's own history. To few writers has the faculty been given in measure so rich of projecting objectively the scenes he was describing upon some outward, yet imaginary canvas, whence he transferred them to his pages. The naturalness of setting in the case of all the incidents is so marked, and stands out in such glaring contrast to those recorded in the *Memoirs of a Lady of Quality* (published in *Peregrine Pickle*), that one scarcely knows which to admire most—the originality of the genius or the wonderful fidelity and impressiveness of the painter's reproduction.

Smollett's strength lay in his great power of self–restraint. He knew what he could do, and with rare wisdom he kept himself within the limits of his imaginative ability. He could very easily have made either Roderick Random or Peregrine Pickle a sentimental amorist, sighing after his mistress, and suffering all the delicious hopes and fears and ups and downs of the knights–errant of love. But therein he would have trenched upon Richardson's province, and placed himself in a decidedly unfavourable comparison with the author of *Pamela* and *Clarissa Harlowe*. He might have developed a splendid character–study out of the colossal Borgia–like wickedness of Ferdinand Count Fathom, who can alone claim kindred, in the pitiless thirst for crime which possesses him, with that repulsively brutal creation of

Shakespeare's early days, Aaron in *Titus Andronicus*, who, when dying, curses the world with the words—

'If one good deed in all my life I did,
I do repent it from my very soul.'

But had he done so, he would have entered into direct competition with Fielding; a competition he knew he was unfitted to support. But in his own department he was supreme. In fertility of invention and apt adaptation of means to end he had no rival. His novels present one bewildering succession of accidents, entanglements, escapes, imprisonments, love–makings, and what not, until the mind positively becomes cloyed with the banquet of incident provided for it. A less profound genius than Smollett would in all probability have worn itself out in a vain attempt to rival his great contemporaries, on the principle 'never venture, never win.' Smollett was a surer critic, on this point at least, than many of his friends, who were continually urging him to attempt something in the mode of Fielding. 'There is but one husbandman can reap that field,' he replied. He knew what he *could* do and what he *could not* do, and therein, as has been said, lay his strength.

Viewing his novels as a whole,—*Roderick Random, Peregrine Pickle, Ferdinand Count Fathom, Launcelot Greaves, The Adventures of an Atom*, and *Humphrey Clinker*,—the first quality which strikes a critical reader is the family likeness existing between all the leading characters. Dissimilar though Roderick Random and Ferdinand Count Fathom may be in their impulses toward evil, distinct though Peregrine Pickle is from Launcelot Greaves, Matthew Bramble, and Lismahago in what may be termed his nobler qualities, there is nevertheless in all that happy–go–lucky carelessness, that supreme indifference to consequences, that courage that never flinches from the penalties of its own misdeeds, but accepts them without a murmur—in a word, a *bonhomie* diversified by egotism, that appears in equal measure in no other novelist of his time. Richardson displays that sentimental, melodramatic, watery 'gush' which the taste of last century denominated pathos—the sort of thing Dickens long after described in the phrase 'drawing tears from his eyes and a handkerchief from his pocket'; but of that quality there is not the faintest trace in Smollett. If anything, his characters are too callous, too fond of the rough–and–tumble Tom–and–Jerry life in which their creator so perceptibly revelled. Fielding, on the other hand, patiently elaborates his characters, adding here a line and there a curve, heightening the light in one place, deepening the shading in another, never picturing an incident or a trait without some definite end to be served in perfecting the final portrait. Smollett never takes time for such microscopic character studies. He is a veritable pen–and–ink draughtsman. With bold, rapid, vigorous strokes, he sketches, through the agency of incident, the outlines of his characters, filling in these outlines with but few subsidiary details regarding the feelings and moral impulses of his creations. For such he has neither the time nor the space. Let any reader lift the conceptions of Roderick Random, or Peregrine Pickle, or Matthew Bramble out of the setting of the story and study them apart, paying no heed to anything affecting the other personages, and he will see at once how completely Smollett relied on incident to do the work of explaining and analysing the feelings of his heroes. Fielding was the greater artist, Smollett the better story–teller; Fielding was the greater moral teacher, Smollett the more vigorous painter of contemporary manners. Further, let the reader carefully study Lovelace in Richardson's *Clarissa Harlowe*, Blifil in Fielding's novel of *Tom Jones*, and Smollett's Ferdinand Count Fathom, and he will perceive in even a stronger degree the diverse method of the three great novelists. Richardson builds up what might be called the 'architectonic' of the creation by a series of great scenes wherein dialogue plays the greatest part. Lovelace has all the light–hearted villainy of a man to whom virtue is a myth, who has no conscience, and whose standard of right is his gross animal devilishness. Richardson does everything by square and rule. He expends at the outset a wealth of ingenuity in portraying the most insignificant qualities of Lovelace's nature. And so fully does he make us acquainted with his nature, that at the end of the novel we know in reality very little more of him than we did at the outset. Fielding, on the other hand, winds his way into the very heart of a character, 'like a serpent round its prey,' as Goldsmith said of Burke's treatment of a subject in conversation. Every chapter gives us some addition to the creation, even to the very close of the novel. But when that is reached, the great synthesis is complete. Not a trait is lacking, and Master Blifil stands pilloried to all time as the type of everything that is contemptible and deceitful. Not so Smollett. In the case of Ferdinand Count Fathom the initial description of the character is reduced to a minimum. Everything is left to the effect produced by incident. All Fathom's pitilessness, his absolute love of vice for its own sake, his colossal selfishness, are in reality merely suggested to the reader's own mind, by the thread of rapidly succeeding incident, not formally labelled as such. In the case of both Richardson and Fielding the author is constantly present in his creation. So with Smollett, he is ever in evidence. None of them attain that superb art of Walter Scott, who simply effaces himself in his creations, or, as Hazlitt says: 'He sits like a magician in his cell and conjures up all shapes and sights to the view; but in the midst of all this phantasmagoria the author himself never appears to take part with his characters. It is the perfection of art to conceal art, and this is here done so completely, that, while it adds to our pleasure in the work, it seems to take away from the merit of the author. As he does not thrust himself into the foreground, he loses the credit of the performance.'

By the critical student closely attentive to the development of Smollett's genius, the fact will assuredly be noted that in the gallery of his characters, chronologically considered, there is a definitely progressive growth or increase in the power wherewith he limned character. Bearing in mind our initial position, that in Smollett's art incident was the prime element, and the delineation of character subordinate to the artistic arrangement of the links in the chain of circumstance, I would invite attention to the following analysis, as being, in my opinion, the conclusion to be deduced from a patient, faithful, and impartial study of the personages named. My contention is that in the character sequence we have a series of ascending psychologic gradations, each one presenting features of greater complexity and philosophic force, as the author realised more clearly the value of a system in that concatenation of event which influenced so intimately his personages.

Roderick Random is little else than the *Gil Blas* of Le Sage Anglified, with some hints borrowed from the excellent *Lazarillo de Tormes* of Hurtado de Mendoza. In his Preface to the novel Smollett acknowledges his indebtedness to French and Spanish fiction, and announces his conviction of the superiority of the novel of circumstance over all others. *Roderick Random*, therefore, as a novel consists of a succession of incidents, some startling, some improbable, some foolish, and some highly effective, but all loosely strung together without much artistic arrangement or relative affinity to each other. The book is a record of the 'adventures' of the hero from his cradle to his marriage. As in the case of all such books, the peg whereon the incidents are hung is very slender. All is loose and disjointed, happy–go–lucky in narration, rapid, swift, and evanescent in the mental pictures produced. Roderick is only a big schoolboy, full of animal spirits and animal passions, far, very far from being a saint, yet as far from being an irreclaimable sinner. He is the plaything of his passions, carried like a straw on the stream of circumstance. He takes everything as it comes, be it weal be it woe, be it good fortune or evil, with supreme nonchalance. He shows little regard or gratitude to his uncle, Lieutenant Bowling. He treats his poor friend Strap, whose only fault was his fidelity, worse than indifferently. He is not by any means faithful, and certainly not very respectful, to his lady–love, Narcissa; nay, he even takes the discovery of his long–lost father—a circumstance materially altering his social station—quite as a matter of course. Roderick Random was the spirit incarnate of the cold–blooded, coarse–fibred, religionless eighteenth century—a century wherein virtue was perpetually on the lips, and vice as perpetually in the hearts of its men, a century wherein its women were colourless puppets, without true individuality or definite aims, but oscillating aimlessly between Deism and Methodism to escape from the ennui that resulted from the lack of true culture. Roderick Random as a creation was a purely adventitious one, resulting from the fortuitous concourse of incidents. How the character was to shape itself, morally or mentally, seemed to trouble the creator little, provided the events were sufficiently lively and brisk, and the interest in the story was maintained unflaggingly. Incidents were piled up, whether tending to heighten the effect of the *dramatis personæ*, or not. There was no conservation of material, no wise economy, no evidence of careful selection. Prodigality and profusion were everywhere present, with the signs of youth and inexperience writ large over all. In fact, the character of Roderick Random, critically estimated as a work of art, is little better than Lobeyra's Amadis de Gaul, a portrait limned wholly out of incident, flung on the canvas without premeditation, and frequently presenting inconsistencies and conflicting traits. There is no gradual development of character contemporaneously with the evolution of event. The character has gathered no wisdom during its course. It is represented to us in quite as immature a state at the end of the story as at the beginning. There is a heartlessness, a moral callousness about Roderick which all his experiences never seemed to remove. Excessively repulsive is this phase of the hero's character; nay, the novel is only saved from being as darkly shaded and as morally repellent as Count Fathom, by the pathetic doglike fidelity of poor Strap, who exhibits more true nobility of nature in a chapter, than Roderick Random in the whole book.

From the criticisms on *Roderick Random*, Smollett learned many lessons. He noted that, though his free and easy method of letting character shape itself through the medium of incident had its advantages, these were liable to be counterbalanced unless the chain of incident was so forged that each link would be related to the leading characters of the novel, so as to promote their development and tend to fill in the bare black and white outlines by some distinguishing trait, mannerism, or eccentricity. In *Peregrine Pickle*, therefore, the characters are seen to be more vertebrate. They are no longer the stalking lay figures of the first novel. Albeit Peregrine is only Roderick under another name, and endowed with a year or two more of experience and sense,—the subtle differentiation of personages visible in *Humphrey Clinker* having yet to be learned,—there is a marked improvement in the *technique* of the novel. The chain of incident is every whit as varied, the events as events are more stirring and startling than in the first novel, but there is now the attempt—though as yet but an attempt—to subject the unflagging flow of incident to an artistic adaptation towards definite ends. Incident is no longer piled on incident regardless of the fact whether it tend to advance the development of the characters or not. Then Smollett has learned the value of contrast in character–painting. Peregrine is contrasted with such humorous creations as Godfrey Gauntlet, Commodore Hawser Trunnion, Lieutenant Hatchway, and Bo'sun Tom Pipes. The virtue of relative proportion among his characters according to their ratio of importance in influencing the story, though still faulty, has been carefully studied. Peregrine therefore is supreme as hero. There is no Strap to dispute the honours with him, and as a portrait he is more consistent than in the case of Roderick. Though the same callous indifference to morality is manifest, though the likeness to Lazarillo de Tormes is even more patent in this latter creation than in the former, though the same polite villainy passes current under the name of gallantry, the same cheap appreciation of female honour,—witness that degrading scene so reprobated by Sir Walter Scott, where Peregrine assails Emilia Gauntlet's chastity,—the hero is not so glaring a moral imbecile as Roderick. He has gleams of better things. But, as in the former novel so in the latter, the noblest character of the book is the foil or contrast to Peregrine—Godfrey Gauntlet, on whom Smollett seems to lavish all his powers.

Then comes *Ferdinand Count Fathom*, indicating a still further advance in the *technique* of novel–writing. In this work the stage is not so crowded as in *Roderick Random* and *Peregrine Pickle*. The whole interest centres in the career of crime of this archfiend, this pitiless Nero, Iago, and Cæsar Borgia in one. A more terrible picture of human depravity has never been drawn unless in *Othello* and *Titus Andronicus*. But Smollett had now learned the lesson of the conservation of imaginative power. There are no needless incidents in this novel. Everyone reveals the character of the hero in a new light. Relative proportion, differentiation, and contrast have all been carefully studied. Notwithstanding our loathing of crimes so unspeakable, notwithstanding our hatred of animalism so unbridled as would sacrifice the trustful Monimia to his base passions, a sort of sneaking sympathy with Fathom begins to find entrance into the breast. As in *Paradise Lost* one feels a sorrow for Satan's position after his magnificent resistance to the Almighty, so here the same sentiment finds place. One hopes Fathom may have time given him wherein to repent. But Smollett was now too consummate an artist for that concession to sentimentalism. In *Roderick Random* he might have committed such an artistic mistake. Not now. Fathom receives retributive justice, and only repents when he has expiated to the uttermost his sins and wrong–doings.

Passing by *Sir Launcelot Greaves* and *The History of an Atom* as outside the pale of our criticism, inasmuch as they were written when he was worried and distracted with other matters, besides being in wretched health, so that they are unworthy of his genius, we come to the consideration of Matthew Bramble and Lieutenant Lismahago in *Humphrey Clinker*. They are undoubtedly the two greatest characters in the Smollett gallery of imaginative portraits. They must be viewed together. To separate them is to lose the reflected lustre they cast by contrast on each other. Likenesses many and important they have. Both are sufferers from the world's fickle changes. Both are weary and irritated with society's meannesses and petty falsehoods. Both are testy, tetchy, and prickly–tempered. But how truly men! Smollett had now reached the meridian of his powers. He realised now that in a great novel incident and the delineation of character must occupy co–ordinate positions.

To assign excessive predominance to either, is to mar the ultimate effect. Therefore in *Humphrey Clinker*, while still revelling in inexhaustible variety of incident, Smollett assigns to the synthesis of character its proper place. In place of portraying the characters himself, he adopted the course, so favoured by his great rival Richardson, and long years after to be employed with such rare effect by Walter Scott and William Makepeace Thackeray, of achieving the evolution of character through the medium of letters, a mutual analysis as well as a distinctive synthesis. Risky though the expedient was, for it demanded a man of the highest genius to make the letters popular, in Smollett's hands it proved eminently successful. We accordingly have Matthew Bramble alternately described by himself and Jerry Melford, each giving varying phases of the same kindly, dogmatic, generously obstinate, and wholly noble–hearted fellow. Lismahago's character, besides being drawn by the two above–named fellow–travellers in that expedition to Scotland wherein Humphrey Clinker was the footman and hero, has the blanks in the portrait filled in by Miss Tabitha Bramble, the bitter–sweet spinster whom he afterwards married, and the inimitably delightful lady's–maid, Winnifred Jenkins. More highly finished pictures could scarcely be desired. Side by side with Scott's Dugald Dalgetty and Thackeray's Esmond, Lismahago may assuredly be placed, while Matthew Bramble falls little short, in completeness of details, of Jonathan Oldbuck in the *Antiquary*. Yet Bramble is still Roderick Random and Peregrine Pickle purged of their faults and follies, and with the experience of years upon them. We realise that Bramble possesses all their shortcomings, albeit held in check by his strong good sense, while they potentially had all his virtues, though the fever of youth i' the blood obscured them for the nonce. A noble gallery do these five characters compose. If Fathom be the Cain or the Esau of the company, he has many of the family features to show to what race he belongs.

In one imaginative type Smollett has never been approached as a creator, to wit, in his delineation of British seamen. Captain Marryat exhibits a greater knowledge of nautical affairs than Smollett, but nothing in the younger novelist quite touches the racy humour of Commodore Hawser Trunnion, Lieutenant Bowling, Hatchway, and Pipes. David Hannay, in his introduction to *Japhet in Search of a Father*, says: 'Captain Savage of the *Diomede*, Captain M—— of the *King's Own*, Captain Hector Maclean in *Jacob Faithful*, Terence O'Brien, the mate Martin, the midshipman Gascoigne, Thomas Saunders the boatswain's mate, and Swinburne the quartermaster, are beyond all question not less lifelike portraits of the officers and men of the navy than Trunnion and Bowling, Pipes and Hatchway. In one respect Marryat had an inevitable advantage over his predecessor. Smollett never shows us the seaman at his work. He could not, because he did not know it sufficiently well to understand it himself.' That is perfectly true. But, on the other hand, Marryat's intimate knowledge was often a hindrance to his art. It led him to inflict the minutiæ of the service on his readers more than was needful. Hence the reason why some parts of Marryat's books are decidedly tiresome. Smollett's are never so. His sense of artistic proportion was finer than Marryat's, and he avoided the pitfall whereinto the other fell. As a delineator of the nautical character, Mr. Clark Russell is the greatest we have had since Smollett, and in him the latter finds his most dangerous rival. Yet, if Mr. Russell has equalled his master in many other respects, it is doubtful if he has quite reached the high–water mark of Commodore Trunnion and Lismahago.

Finally, Smollett's women are deserving of a word. Sainte Beuve said he judged a novelist's powers by the manner in which he drew his female characters. If so, Smollett would not have excited much sympathy in the mind of the brilliant author of the *Causeries du Lundi*. His women are of varying excellence. Narcissa in *Roderick Random* and Emilia in *Peregrine Pickle* are only sweet dolls. Until his closing years he could not differentiate between puling sentimentality and piquancy. Into the charming perversity, the delightful contradictoriness, that often make up for us one–half the attractiveness of the female character, he could not enter. To rise to the height of spiritual insight that was requisite to conceive and execute a Di Vernon, an Ethel Newcome, or a Rose Vincy, was for him impossible, simply because he could not realise in his earlier years of authorship that women are the equals, not the inferiors of man. The hapless Miss Williams in *Roderick Random* exhibits this feeling on the part of Smollett. She was nobility itself in character, yet she was made over to Strap. One of the finest of his creations is the hapless Monimia in *Count Fathom*. Tenderness, purity, grace, and beauty are all united in her. She falls, it is true, but her fall left her virtue unimpugned, seeing that her betrayer resorted to means as cruel as they were irresistible to accomplish his diabolic purpose. Monimia occupies a pedestal apart, but, she excepted, the two most delightful creations in all his works are those in *Humphrey Clinker*, Tabitha Bramble and Winnifred Jenkins. Lydia Melford is too milk–and–waterish, but the two first–named are drawn with masterly precision and force. Tabitha Bramble is a capital portrait of the soured, disappointed old maid, whose lover had died long before, but to whose memory she had been ever faithful—a woman whose nature is only encrusted with prejudice, not inter–penetrated by it, so that we may justly hope that, under the loving care of Lieutenant Lismahago, her frigidity may thaw, and that in matrimony she may discover the world not to be so very bad after all. Winnifred Jenkins is the prototype of Mrs. Malaprop in Sheridan's *Rivals*, and is infinitely more amusing. All the vanity, self–assertiveness, and jealousy of a small mind, conjointly with the love of appearing to move in a higher circle of society than she really does, are admirably sketched, while her misappropriate use of the language of that circle is most felicitously rendered. The portrait is Smollett's best, and no touch is finer than Winnifred's conduct in the menagerie. Let her speak for herself. 'Last week I went with mistress to the Tower to see the crowns and wild beastis. There was a monstracious lion with teeth half a quarter long, and a gentleman bid me not go near him if I wasn't a maid, being as how he would roar, and tear, and play the dickens. Now I had no mind to go near him, for I cannot abide such dangerous honeymils, not I—but mistress would go, and the beast kept such a roaring and bouncing that I tho't he would have broke his cage and devoured us all; and the gentleman tittered forsooth; but I'll go death upon it, I will, that my lady is as good a firgkin as the child unborn; and therefore either the gentleman told a phib, or the lion ought to be set in the stocks for bearing false witness against his neighbour.' Tabitha Bramble and Win Jenkins are those two in Smollett's gallery of fiction which the world will not willingly let die.

Such, then, is Smollett as a novelist—the great master of incident and humorous narration, the painter of the faults, foibles, and eccentricities of his fellow–men. In his own sphere he was unrivalled, and he in nothing showed more saliently his good sense than by refusing to attempt works for which he knew he was both by temperament and training unfitted. I cannot quite agree with Professor Saintsbury's view in his charming and sympathetic Life of Smollett, prefixed to what bids fair to be the standard edition of his works.[10] 'The only one of the deeper and higher passions which seems to have stirred Smollett was patriotism, in which a Scot rarely fails, unless he is an utter gaby or an utter scoundrel.' Does not the worthy Professor, following the popular definition, fail to differentiate between an *emotion* and a *passion*. In depicting the passions, Smollett, I grant, was singularly deficient; in such emotions as patriotism, sympathy with the oppressed, and a pure devotion to the cause of truth, he showed himself a man whose heart was permeated with the warmest and deepest enthusiasm.

CHAPTER XI

SMOLLETT AS HISTORIAN AND CRITIC

A hundred and thirty years ago, if one had been asked to name the six great historians then alive, Smollett with marked unanimity would have been mentioned amongst the first. In fact, Hume, Robertson, and he were then reckoned as the illustrious triumvirate of Scots whose genius, in default of others native born, had been consecrated to the task of lauding for bread and fame the annals of the land whose glories were supposed to be to them so distasteful. The Union of the countries was not yet sufficiently remote to have borne as its fruit that harvest of commercial, political, and agricultural benefits that have accrued to both lands as its result. The jealousy wherewith Scotsmen were regarded in England was a legacy from the days when the subjugation of the territory north of Tweed was a standing item in English foreign policy, from the reign of that greatly misjudged monarch, Edward I. (Longshanks), to the days of the fourth of his name, who recognised the younger brother of James III., the exiled Duke of Albany, as King of Scots under the title of Alexander IV., on condition that he acknowledged Edward as lord paramount and feudal superior.

The school of historians represented by Rapin, Oldmixon, Tindal, Carte, and Hooke, honest, hard–working investigators, but without any sense of method or proportion in classifying or arranging materials, and vigorous anti–Scots, was alarmed by the success attending the publication of Hume's *History of England* in 1754–61, Principal Robertson's *History of Scotland* in 1758–59, and Smollett's *History of England* in 1758. When the Continuation by the last–named appeared in 1762, it was exposed, as we have seen, to a perfect broadside of misrepresentation and unjust reflections, prompted by the historians above–named and their booksellers, whose literary property seemed to them to be endangered. That some of the criticisms were just, and founded upon the discovery of genuine errors and blemishes in the history, cannot be denied. But, on the other hand, three–fourths of the allegations were baseless, because proceeding from spleen, and not from genuine enthusiasm in the cause of historic truth.

For example, the objections urged by the friends and supporters of Rapin's History were that Smollett was too hurried in his survey, that he took too many facts on trust, that he was unfair in his critical estimates of eminent personages, and finally, that his style was one better adapted for the novel than for historical compositions. To these allegations the friends of Oldmixon added that he permitted party prejudice to colour all his judgments. In replying to such charges we virtually analyse Smollett's merits as a historian. A double duty is therefore discharged by so doing.

Smollett as a historian might say with Horace, and assuredly with truth, '*Nullius addictus jurare in verba magistri*—a slavish disciple of the tenets of no master am I.' Though unstinted in his praise of Hume's calm, lucid survey, of his careful generalisations and eminently comprehensive method, though likewise a generous admirer of Robertson's brilliant word–pictures and glowingly eloquent narrative, wherein the long dead seemed to live again, he had his own ideal of the writing of history, and it savoured rather of Tacitus than of Thucydides. His method consisted in presenting a series of great outstanding events covering the entire period under notice, and round these to group the subordinate occurrences either resulting from or happening contemporaneously with them. He was a firm believer in the doctrine that political freedom and commercial honesty are the two great bulwarks of any State. Though a Tory in name, he was in reality more of a philosophical Whig, rather a champion of the rights of the people than a lover and defender of aristocracies, oligarchies, and monopolies. 'That country only is truly prosperous that is in the highest sense free, and that country alone is free where a hierarchy of knowledge governs, uninfluenced by faction and undisturbed by prejudice,' he wrote in the *Critical Review*. The sentiments are somewhat vague and indefinite, but they show that he was striving to emancipate himself from the leading–strings of party prejudice.

Although the fact is beyond doubt that Smollett's historical works were written exceedingly rapidly, on the other hand, we must remember that the rapidity of production merely applied to the mechanical work of transcribing what had been already carefully thought out. Like Dr. Johnson, Smollett was possessed of a most retentive memory. He rarely committed any of his works to paper until he had thoroughly thought them out in his mind, and had tested them over and over again in that searching alembic. In neither case, therefore, was the *composition* hurried. All that was done was to expedite its transcription. Smollett's historical judgments, in place of being hastily formed, were the result of patient study and thought. On this point we have the evidence of Wilkes, who, in one of his epigrams, more forcible than delicate, remarked that Smollett travailed over the birth of his historical judgments so much that he (Wilkes) had often to play the part of the critical midwife.

The next charge, that Smollett was too prone to take his information at second hand, cannot be altogether controverted, though it was not yet the custom of historians to betake themselves to the MS. repositories of the country for their materials. More mutual reliance was placed by historians on each other's *bonâ fides* and faculty of critical selection than seems to be the case now. But we have it on his own assurance that he consulted over three hundred authorities for his facts. That number may be small compared with those eight hundred names which Buckle prints at the commencement of his noble and imperishable *History of Civilisation in England*, but in Smollett's day the number of his references was considered phenomenal. He greatly surpassed Hume in the range and appropriateness of his references, and rather prided himself on the collateral evidences of facts which he was able to adduce from his miscellaneous reading. That Smollett was consciously unfair in his judgment of any character in his historical works cannot be credited. He was too warm a friend of truth to be seduced into wilfully distorting the plain and straightforward deductions from ascertained facts. That he may have been misled I do not deny, that his political predilections may have led him insensibly to colour his judgments at times with the jaundice of partisanship, is quite possible, yet that such was done deliberately, no student of Smollett's character for a moment will credit. Many of his political opponents were castigated, it is true, so were many of his political friends; but, on the other hand, the fact is to be taken into account that many of his bitterest enemies obtained a just and impartial criticism from Smollett when such was denied to them by many of the writers numbered among their own friends. Finally, that his style was more adapted to the treatment of imaginative themes than of sober historical narrative, was a charge that might have some weight in the middle decades of last century. It can have none now. No special style is distinctively to be employed in historical composition. It affords scope for all. True it is that Echard and his school, in the early decades of the eighteenth century, contended that history should be written in a style of sober commonplace altogether divested of ornament, as thereby the judgment was not likely to be led astray. But such nonsensical reservations have long since been relegated to the limbo of exploded theories, and in historical composition the brilliancy of a Macaulay and of an Alison finds a place as well as the sober sense of a Hallam or a Stubbs; the picturesqueness of a Froude, as well as the earnest vigour and tireless industry of a Freeman. Smollett's style, so nervous, pointed, and epigrammatic, so full of strength and beauty as well as of scintillating sparkle, was somewhat of a surprise in his day. Hume's easy, flowing, pithy Saxon, and Robertson's stately splendour, had both carried the honours in historical composition to the grey metropolis of the North. The fact that another Scot, albeit resident in London, should repeat the success, and in some respects excel both, was the most crushing blow the elder school of history had received. Thenceforward we hear nothing of them. Rapin and Oldmixon slumbered with the spiders on the remotest shelves of the great libraries. Their day was past. A new school of British historians had arisen.

Smollett's historical works, his *History of England*, his *Continuation of the History of England*, his *Histories of France, Italy, and Germany*, are characterised by the following sterling qualities:—a felicity of method whereby the narrative flows on easily and consecutively from beginning to end, and whereby, through its division into chapters, representing definite epochs, one is able to discover with ease any specific point that may be desired; an exhibition of the principles whereon just and equitable government should proceed, namely, that of a limited monarchy; a judicious subordination of the less to the more important events in the narrative; short, pithy, but eminently fair and appreciative criticisms of all the more outstanding personages in the country under treatment, and a convincing testimony borne to the axiom that only by national virtue and the conservation of national honour can any nation either reach greatness or retain it. If Smollett did not possess Hume's power of reaching back to first principles in tracing the evolution of a country's greatness, or Robertson's stimulating eloquence that fired the heart with noble sentiments, he had the virtue, scarcely less valuable, of keeping more closely to his theme than either of them, and of producing works that read like a romance. If Hume were the superior in what may be styled the philosophy of history, if Robertson in picturesqueness and eloquence, Smollett was the better narrator of the circumstances and facts as they actually occurred. In many respects he resembles Diderot, and the analogy is not lessened when we compare the private lives of the two men. To Smollett history was only of value insomuch as we are able to read the present by the key of the past, and to influence the future by avoiding the mistakes of the past and present. Smollett was a patriot in the broad catholic signification of the word. He had no sympathy with the patriotism that is synonymous with national or racial selfishness. More crimes have stained the annals of humanity under the guise of patriotism than can be atoned for by cycles of penitence. To Smollett the soul of patriotism was summed up in sinking the name of Scot in the generic one of Briton, and in endeavouring to stamp out that pitiful provincialism that considered one's love of country to be best manifested in perpetuating quarrels whereon the mildew of centuries had settled. Smollett in his historical works showed himself a truer patriot than that. Though a leal–hearted Scot, he was likewise a magnanimous–spirited Briton, ready to judge as he would wish to be judged. Writing of the Union of 1707, he remarks in his Continuation: 'The majority of both nations believed that the treaty would produce violent convulsions, or, at best, prove ineffectual. But we now see it has been attended with none of the calamities that were prognosticated, that it quietly took effect, and answered all the purposes for which it was intended. Hence we may learn that many great difficulties are surmounted because they are not seen by those who direct the execution of any great project; and that many great schemes which theory deems impracticable will yet succeed in the experiment.'

Some critics have urged that Smollett might have taken a broader view of the sources and progress of national expansion and development. Minto rather off–handedly designates his style as 'fluent and loose, possessing a careless vigour where the subject is naturally exciting,' and concluding with the words, 'the history *is said* to be full of errors and inconsistencies.'[11] Now, this last clause is taken word for word from Chambers's *Cyclopedia of English Literature*, who took it from Angus's *English Literature*, who borrowed it from Macaulay, who annexed it from the *Edinburgh Review*, which journal had originally adopted it with alterations from Smollett's own prefatory remarks in the first edition of the book. How many of these authors had read the history for themselves, to see if it really contained such errors and inconsistencies? Criticism conducted on that mutual–trust principle is very convenient for the critic; is it quite fair to the author? Now, anyone who faithfully reads Smollett's *History of England* and its *Continuation* will not discover a larger percentage of either errors or inconsistencies than appear in the works of his contemporary historians, Tytler, Hume, and Robertson. Smollett is as distinguishingly fair and impartial as it was possible for one to be, influenced so profoundly by his environment as were all the historians of the eighteenth century. The mind of literary Europe was already tinged by that spiritual unrest and moral callousness that was to induce the new birth of the French Revolution.

As a literary critic, during his tenure of the editorial chair of the *Critical Review*, Smollett's judgments were frequently called in question, especially in the case of Dr. Grainger, the translator of *Tibullus* and of the Greek dramatists, and author of the *Ode to Solitude*; Shebbeare, a well–known political writer of the period, whose seditious utterances had been chastised; Home, the author of *Douglas*, and Wilkie of the *Epigoniad*. Now, in nearly all the cases wherein exception was taken to the articles, these were not written by Smollett. But even as regards those of his own composition that have been complained of, careful perusal alike of the volume criticised and of the critique evince Smollett to have been as just and fair in the circumstances as he could well be. For example, the opinion he formed of Churchill's Poems was that in which the British public within thirty years was to acquiesce,—nay, is that which to–day is the prevailing literary verdict upon these once popular works. Smollett unfortunately left his contributors a perfectly free hand. Many of them were men of no principle, who permitted private grudges to colour their critical estimate of literary works produced by those with whom they had some quarrel or disagreement. Smollett was to blame for not exercising his editorial scissors more freely on the verdicts of his *collaborateurs*. His own opinions of current literature were expressed with a fairness leaving little to be desired. Though not a Sainte Beuve in critical appreciation of the work of others, though his verdicts never possessed the keen spiritual and emotional insight of the famous *Causeries du Lundi* in the Paris *Constitutional*, still they are the fair, honest, outspoken opinions of a man who, as Morton said of Knox, 'never feared the face of man,' and therefore would not be biassed by favour or fear. Dr. Johnson was at the same time criticising literature in his new *Literary Magazine*. Interesting it is to compare the two opinions on the books they dealt with. Smollett's style is well–nigh as distinguishable as Johnson's among his fellow–contributors. If the decrees of 'the Great Cham of Literature'[12] are more authoritative, they are but little more incisive and searching than those of the author of *Roderick Random*. The former had a more extensive vocabulary, the latter was the more consummate literary critic. Wit, humour, pathos, and epigram were all at the service of Smollett, and though, in depth of thought and soaring sublimity of reasoning powers, the author of the *Rambler* excelled his contemporary, in the lighter graces of style Smollett was the better of the two. Though he had not

Johnson's Jove–like power of driving home a truth, he frequently persuaded, by his calm and lucid logic, where the thunder of the Great Cham only repelled. If blame be his, then, with regard to the exercise of his critical authority, it was due more to sins of omission than of commission, more to believing that others were actuated by the same high ideals in criticism as himself. In reading some of the numbers of the *Critical Review* for the purposes of this biography, nothing struck me more in those papers that were plainly from the pen of Smollett, than the power he possessed of placing himself at the point of view assumed by the writer of the work under criticism, so that he might be thoroughly *en rapport* with the author's sympathies. How few critics have either the inclination or the ability to do likewise!

CHAPTER XII

SMOLLETT AS POET AND DRAMATIST

Tradition states that Smollett, on being asked on one occasion why he did not write more poetry, replied that he had 'no time to be a poet.' The answer can be read in a dual sense—either that poetry demanded an absorption so complete in its pursuit that all other interests were as naught; or, on the other hand, that his time was so fully occupied that he could not devote attention to poetical composition without neglecting other things at that time of more value. As weighed against his fiction, little regret can be felt by any admirer of Smollett, that he did not pursue poetry more diligently. The specimens we possess of these fruits of his genius are not of such value as to awaken any desire to peruse more of his metrical essays. Small in bulk though his poetical works are, even these, as well as his dramatic compositions, we would gladly have spared in exchange for such another novel as *Humphrey Clinker*.

Smollett's genius was by no means of that purely imaginative, highly spiritual type from which great poetical compositions are to be expected. He was rather an unsurpassed observer, who, having noted special characteristics of mind as being produced by the fortuitous concourse of certain incidents, straightway proceeded to expand and idealise them; than a mighty original genius, like Shakespeare, Milton, Spenser, Shelley, or Keats, that from the depths of his spiritual consciousness evolved original creations that are representative not of any age, but of all time. Smollett had none of the isolating power of the true poet, whereby for the time he raises his theme into the pure ether of imagination, dissociated from the world and all its concerns. Smollett loved the world too well to seek to sever himself from it. His workshop, his studio, his school, and observatory, it was in one. Like Balzac, he was more taken up with what men did than with what they thought. From the outward evidence of action he worked back to the predisposing thought, not predicting *à priori* from the thought what the action must necessarily be. Therefore, as Smollett's genius was more practical than imaginative, dealing more with the reproduction of facts than the creation of fancies, his poetry rose little above the dead level of commonplace. Only in two poems does he rise into a distinctively higher altitude of poetic inspiration—these are 'The Tears of Scotland' and 'The Ode to Independence.' In both cases, however, the influence of patriotism and that keen sympathy with the oppressed which he always entertained, contributed to impart to the compositions in question loftier sentiments and more impassioned feelings than would otherwise have been the case. We have already seen that the horrors wrought in the Jacobite Rebellion of 1745 by the Duke of Cumberland were on his mind when he wrote 'The Tears of

Scotland'; while the heroism of the noble Corsican Paschal Paoli was the stimulating motive in the composition of the latter.

There is a great difference between the two. The former was written in 1746, while the 'Ode to Independence' was not produced until the last years of his life, and was not published until 1773, when the Messrs. Foulis of Glasgow, printers to the University of Glasgow, put it out, with a short Preface and Notes by Professor Richardson. In both, the language is spirited and striking, the thoughts elevated and just. In the 'Ode' he takes as his models Collins and Gray. The first and last stanzas of it—or, more properly, the opening strophe and the concluding antistrophe—are the finest in the poem, and are well worthy of quotation—

'Thy spirit, Independence, let me share,
Lord of the lion–heart and eagle eye:
Thy steps I follow with my bosom bare,
Nor heed the storm that howls along the sky.
Deep in the frozen regions of the North,
A goddess violated brought thee forth,
Immortal Liberty, whose look sublime
Hath bleached the tyrant's cheek in ever–varying clime.
What time the iron–hearted Gaul,
With frantic Superstition for his guide,
Armed with the dagger and the pall,
The Sons of Woden to the field defied;
The ruthless hag by Weser's flood
In Heaven's name urged the infernal blow,
And red the stream began to flow,
The vanquished were baptised with blood.

ANTISTROPHE.

Nature I'll court in her sequestered haunts
By mountain, meadow, streamlet, grove or cell,
Where the poised lark his evening ditty chants,
And Health and Peace and Contemplation dwell.
There Study shall with Solitude recline,
And Friendship pledge me to his fellow–swains;
And Toil and Temperance sedately twine
The slender cord that fluttering life sustains:
And fearless Poverty shall guard the door,
And Taste unspoiled the frugal table spread,
And Industry supply the frugal store,
And Sleep unbribed his dews refreshing shed;
White–mantled Innocence, ethereal sprite,

Shall chase afar the goblins of the night,
And Independence o'er the day preside:
Propitious power! my patron and my pride.'

His two satires, *Advice* and *Reproof*, evince on the part of their author the qualities we have already noted—keen power of observation, a felicitous deftness in wedding sound to sense, considerable force of satiric presentation, with humour and wit in rich measure. But there is no such elevation as we discover in Johnson's *London* or *The Vanity of Human Wishes*, or in the satiric pieces of Pope or Dryden. The moment the poems rise from the consideration of facts to principles, Smollett becomes tedious and prosy. As a song–writer, however, he has made some eminently successful essays, the well–known lyric—

'To fix her: 'twere a task as vain
To combat April drops of rain,'

which has been so often set to music, having been written by him soon after the publication of *Roderick Random*. It possesses grace, point, and rhythmic harmony—the three great desiderata in a good lyric. The following verse has a faint echo of the subtle beauty of Wither, Lovelace, Herrick, and the Cavalier poets:—

'She's such a miser eke in love,
Its joys she'll neither share nor prove,
Though crowds of gallants gay await
From her victorious eyes their fate.'

Of his remaining poems there are only one or two that really merit notice. Smollett was too apt to run into the opposite extreme from sacrificing sense to sound, and prefer a repelling roughness both in metre and assonance to altering the sequence of thought in a poem that would not have been injured by the change. His Odes to Mirth and to Sleep are marred by being too didactic. His images are frequently so recondite as to awaken no corresponding ideas in the mind of the reader. His 'Love Elegy' is in imitation of those of Tibullus, and there are several lines that are well–nigh as tenderly pathetic as those of its great original, while the verses 'On a Young Lady playing on the Harpsichord,' so much admired by Sir Walter Scott, are undoubtedly amongst his finest efforts for happy union of glowing thought and graceful expression—

'When Sappho struck the quivering wire,
The throbbing breast was all on fire;
And when she raised the vocal lay,
The captive soul was charmed away:
But had the nymph possessed with these

Thy softer, chaster power to please,
Thy beauteous air of sprightly youth,
Thy native smiles of artless truth,
The worm of grief had never preyed
On the forsaken, love–sick maid;
Nor had she mourned an hapless flame,
Nor dashed on rocks her tender frame.'

Had Smollett cultivated the art of metrical expression more persistently and enthusiastically, there are sufficient indications to show that he might have produced work which, if not in the very highest grade of excellence in the school presided over by Collins, Gray, and Goldsmith, would have attained a standard sufficiently worthy to be ranked among the minor products of that decidedly prosaic epoch. We need not regret his abstention.

Finally, in the drama Smollett's restless genius sought expression at two periods of his life when his hopes were at their highest. In his nineteenth year, we have seen that the fruit of his historical studies, and his wanderings in the glorious Elizabethan drama, had been given to the world in *The Regicide*—a drama founded on the murder of James I. of Scotland. Written at that point in a youth's life when the Will o' the Wisp of literary fame seemed an angel of light, when the prizes incident on intellectual eminence had only recently attracted his gaze, and when his judgment, therefore, was dazzled by the expectation of reaching such a reputation as his countrymen Thomson, Mallet, and Arbuthnot had already won, it had all the faults though but few of the merits of a youthful production. The other piece, *The Reprisal; or, The Tars of Old England*, was executed when his fame was assured, when he was no longer the tyro in composition, but the editor of the *Critical Review* and a critic of the works of others. It is widely different from the *Regicide*, both in style, method, motive, and execution. Yet a beginner in the work of criticism could detect that both were written by the same hand. *The Regicide*, as a drama, is, as we have already said, a very mediocre production. Dealing with a period of Scottish history where there was scope for the aids of a brilliant historic background and of the customs and costumes of the time, Smollett has availed himself of none of these. The characters of the drama are men and women of the eighteenth century, masquerading in anomalous forms of speech and mysterious lines of action, which no one out of Bedlam would have ever considered befitting a king or his nobility. For example, in the play, in place of the *dramatis personæ* being designated as 'James I., King of Scotland,' and 'Joanna Beaufort, Queen of Scotland,' we have simply 'King' and 'Queen,' while the nobles and conspirators bear such utterly inappropriate and unhistoric names as Angus, Dunbar, Ramsay, Stuart, Grime, and Cattan. The action is spasmodic and jerky, altogether lacking in artistic dramatic dovetailing of incidents into each other and of symmetrical consecutiveness of circumstance. James lacks heroism, dignity, and power; Grime—probably meant for Sir Robert Graham—and Athol are very declamatory villains, who, if they put off as much time in firing off expletives at the real scene of the murder, must inevitably have permitted their victim to escape. We seem to be reading a play of Dekker's or Greene's, so very elementary is the stagecraft displayed in contriving exits and entrances for the personages. The characters are all more or less wooden. They talk in stilted, high–flown language, such as a boy of nineteen would suppose the courtiers of a monarch like James I. to employ. They never for a moment descend from their stilts; and even in dying, Dunbar and Eleonora declaim to the audience in rounded and rhetorical periods. Eleonora philosophises as follows within a second or two of her death:—

'Life has its various seasons as the year;
And after clustering autumn—but I faint,
Support me nearer—in rich harvest's rear
Bleak winter must have lagged. Oh! now I feel
The leaden hand of death lie heavy on me—
Thine image swims before my straining eye,
And now it disappears. Speak—bid adieu
To the lost Eleonora. Not a word?
Not one farewell? Alas, that dismal groan
Is eloquent distress! Celestial powers,
Protect my father; show'r upon his—Oh! [*Dies.*]'

Whereupon Dunbar also replies in similar heroics as death approaches—

'There fled the purest soul that ever dwelt
In mortal clay! I come, my love, I come.
Where now the rosy tincture of these lips!
The smile that grace ineffable diffused!
The glance that smote the soul with silent wonder!
The voice that soothed the anguish of disease'—

After which he also cries 'Oh!' and dies. Now, it is very easy to laugh at all this, and to make fun of the inappropriate 'hifalutin.' But, dangerously near bombast though it is, the scene has a pathetic power in it, which, after discounting all its demerits, brings out the balance on the right side of the ledger of praise and blame. Boyish and immature, full of weak and silly passages as the drama is, there are, nevertheless, portions of it which give presage of the genius lying latent beneath the rant and fustian. Mediocre though the piece be, viewed as a whole, isolated passages and lines could be selected from it of the pure imaginative and intellectual ore,—lines and passages, in fine, that lovers of Smollett's genius treasure in their hearts as worthy of the master. Such a passage as the following, being one of the speeches addressed by Dunbar to Eleonora, is aflame with the fiery glow of supreme passion—

'O thy words

Would fire the hoary hermit's languid soul
With ecstasies of pride! How then shall I,
Elate with every vainer hope that warms
The aspiring thought of youth, thy praise sustain
With moderation? Cruelly benign,
Thou hast adorned the victim; but alas!
Thou likewise giv'st the blow! Though Nature's hand
With so much art has blended every grace
In thy enchanting form, that every eye
With transport views thee, and conveys unseen
The soft infection to the vanquished soul,
Yet wilt thou not the gentle passion own
That vindicates thy sway!'

And this, one of Eleonora's replies to Dunbar, is pervaded by an exquisite pathos, as tender as it is true—

'O wondrous power

Of love beneficent! O generous youth,
What recompense (thus bankrupt as I am)
Shall speak my grateful soul? A poor return
Cold friendship renders to the fervid hope
Of fond desire!'

The Reprisal, on the other hand, is little more than a comedietta. It has all the merits of a light, farcical, after–dinner piece, all the faults of a composition that savours more of froth and folly than aught else. The characters of the lovers, Heartly and Harriet, are lightly etched in; but those of Oclabber, an Irish lieutenant, and Maclaymore, a Scots captain, both in the French service, are drawn with great humour and power. Haulyard the midshipman, Lyon the lieutenant, and Block the sailor, all in the English navy, are spirited creations, designed to represent the seamen of Old England at their best. The incidents of the drama are full of life and movement, and the characters are well contrasted as differentiated types. The language, however, is still somewhat stilted and pedantic, so that one can easily detect, amidst all the fun and frolic of *The Reprisal*, the same hand that executed the dark and gloomy *Regicide*.

And now, with the great body of his work before us, looking back also upon all he did, and thought, and said for the good of his brethren of mankind, what is the ultimate verdict which Time has passed on his life and labours? Secure of his niche in the very front rank of the great fathers of English fiction, Smollett's name and literary legacy are precious possessions in the treasure–house of British fiction. Though he is not a 'Scots novelist' in the restricted sense of the term as applied to the writers of these latter days, he has done much to make Scotsmen proud that their country had produced such a son. The works he has executed are assuredly an imperishable memorial. But even more than they do we cherish the example he has set of stern, unflinching devotion to duty, of an honesty that has never been impugned, and of a mighty love for the welfare and the improvement of his brethren of mankind. Every line he wrote was permeated by this intense love of his fellows, and for the amelioration of the lot of the downtrodden he was ready to face both obloquy and danger. A Scot, in the narrow sense of the word, he cannot be considered. As a Briton he will be loved and cherished by a larger family of readers than would be the case did he only appeal to the sympathies of Scotland and the Scots. But though this is so, it does not lessen the regard wherewith his countrymen regard him. After the inspired singer of 'Auld Langsyne,'—after the mighty magician who created such diverse types as Baron Bradwardine, Vich Ian Vohr, Dominie Sampson, Di Vernon, Halbert Glendinning, Jeannie Deans, Rob Roy, and Dugald Dalgetty,—comes he whose children three—Roderick Random, Peregrine Pickle, and Matthew Bramble—will find readers while our language lasts. Proud though we be as Britons to own such a genius as of our tongue, prouder still are we, as Scots, to hail him as akin to us in blood; and so in a double sense rejoicing in his greatness and his glory, we once more bid him farewell!

FOOTNOTES:

[1] At this school the celebrated George Buchanan had been educated, as Mr. Hume Brown indicates in his life of the Scots Scaliger.

[2] See *Sir James Y. Simpson*, by Eve Blantyre Simpson—'Famous Scots' Series.

[3] This was *The Regicide*. It was originally named 'James i.,' but afterwards changed.

[4] Provost Stewart of Edinburgh was a warm Jacobite, and was suspected of assisting the Prince to capture the town.

[5] *Works of John Home, now first collected, with a Life of the Author by Henry Mackenzie*. London, Cadell, 1810.

[6] See *Minutes Select Society*, Advocates' Library, Edinburgh.

[7] See John Rae's *Adam Smith*.

[8] *The Dawn of Radicalism*.

[9] *Autobiography of the Rev. Dr. Alexander Carlyle, Minister of Inveresk*.

[10] Works of T. G. Smollett, edited by George Saintsbury. London: Gibbings & Co.

[11] *Manual of English Prose Literature*.

[12] The title Smollett gave to Johnson when requesting the aid of Wilkes to free Francis Barber, Johnson's black servant, from service on board the *Stag*. It is the older form of *Khan*.

Milton Keynes UK
Ingram Content Group UK Ltd.
UKHW011124180424
441376UK00004B/198